Artists use paintbrushes, sculptors use chisels, musicians use instruments but poets and preachers use words to beautify what's truthful. This book is a gallery of irresistible truths, life changing principles and the miraculous story of a man that dared to know God in the beauty of his holiness. Get ready to be refreshed! Your glasses' prescription will change!

PASTOR DANIEL ARBOLAEZ
Christ Fellowship, Florida

Pastor Andrew's book is a beautiful piece of writing that propels us deeper into the heart of the Father, brings us face to face with the person of Jesus and alerts us to the continuing move of the Holy Spirit. I truly believe God may have put the "sign" you have been looking for into the words He inspired through Andrew McMillan.

JERRY ANDERSON
President of LA RED

What happens when West Virginia meets Yale University meets Medellín, Colombia… Mucho!!! And it's all outlined in this very charming, revealing, and thought-provoking book. Join the exhilarating and humorous ride as Pastor Andrew details how he traversed national, international and inter-denominational borders and the obstacles he overcame en route to becoming the Godly man and exceptional leader he is today. *The Safest Place on Earth* finally provides us the catalyst in which to experience the transformation from gifted speaker to poignant writer.

TROY A. BUDER
Founder and President of TABu Filmz, LLC
Executive Producer, Disney's *The Queen of Katwe*

Andrew McMillan is an extraordinary man. He and his wife Kathy lead the largest church in Medellín, yet you'd never know it in talking to them, they are so humble. Andrew loves people and people love him; he doesn't take himself seriously and simply lives in the goodness of God. I love this man! *The Safest Place on Earth* is full of stories, and they leak out the miraculous. Stories from his youth and chasing girls.

Stories of encountering God in unusual places. Stories that take us on a journey into God's goodness. If you like to glean wisdom and life experience from great leaders, this is a book you will enjoy!

STEVE LONG
Senior Leader, Catch The Fire Toronto

Because Andrew is my friend, saying that his book is amazing sounds like I'm trying to help my friend out. And although that is true, once you start reading *The Safest Place on Earth* you will realize that even his greatest enemies would have to acknowledge the beauty and the mastery of this book. I have been with Andrew and his family in Medellín on multiple occasions. I have enjoyed his leadership and his fathering. I have also been challenged by his humility and his depth. Now, you get to be exposed to the man and his poetry. To his wild journey and his authentic relationship with Jesus. And maybe, just maybe, you will be challenged like me, to imitate Andrew as he imitates Christ.

¡Bravo mi amigo! Este es un libro que el mundo necesita.

CARLOS A. RODRIGUEZ
Author of *Simply Sonship*, Chief Editor of HappySonship.com

Andrew McMillan's book *The Safest Place on Earth* is one of the most unique and entertaining manuscripts I've read in recent years. It's one man's account of a very real and raw journey to discovering God. I want to re-emphasize real and raw. I've known Andrew for some years now. God is using him and his wife, Kathy, in powerful ways in South America. This story is an invitation to souls who are hungry, thirsty, and searching, not forcing you to make any kind of decision, but painting a truly beautiful picture of a journey to faith.

When testimony is shared, often, people sanitize it. They take out the ugly, they remove the "search" and they disregard all of the details. In other words, the stories begin to sound overly "churchy" and religious. Not this book. It is not off-putting for any audience; only inviting, gently calling you to reconsider life as you know it and embrace the very real possibility that "there must be more."

Wherever you find yourself on the faith journey, I know that Andrew's book will surely bring a smile to your face. If you are a follower of Jesus, then I believe it will call you into some new uncharted territory in your interaction with God. If you are still on the fence about this whole "Jesus thing," this is one of the best books you can possibly read, not because it's trying to convert you or proselytize you, but because it's so warm and inviting. By the time you're finished, I trust you're going to want to know the secret of the man with blue sky in his glasses just like Andrew did.

LARRY SPARKS
Publisher, Destiny Image
Author of *Breakthrough Faith* and co-author of *The Fire That Never Sleeps* with Michael Brown and John Kilpatrick

Andrew McMillan writes as only few gifted people can, bringing up the depths of his heart in prose that allow all of us to sing from the pages of his heart. He points people to new possibilities—for example, "I would like to suggest a new category, the miraculous reality. I have seen cracks in the boring routine of reality. There is light brighter than the sun. There is a quiet voice louder than the constant noise of cities. There is a joy underneath the heaviest sorrows. There are people who smell like heaven…" I was captured by the dedication to his sons, and couldn't put it down. *The Safest Place on Earth* is a gift to you—a gift to enrich your life with new possibilities and new ways to see. Don't miss the gift. It is a spiritual and literary feast.

DR. KERRY WOOD
Author and Pastor, Southlake Equip, Gateway Church, Dallas, Texas

The
SAFEST
PLACE

on Earth

ONE MAN'S PURSUIT OF
THE BLUE SKY OF HEAVEN

W. Andrew McMillan

The Safest Place on Earth
Published by Catch The Fire Books
272 Attwell Drive, Toronto ON M9W 6M3 Canada

Distributed worldwide by Catch The Fire Distribution. Titles may be purchased in bulk; for information, please contact distribution@catchthefire.com.

ISBN 978-1-988450-00-1
Copyright © 2016 W. Andrew McMillan

The Team: Hanna Glover, Marcott Bernarde, Benjamin Jackson, Jonathan Puddle, Steve Long

Editor: Noel Gruber

Cover & layout design: Marcott Bernarde

Interior layout: Medlar Publishing Solutions Pvt Ltd, India

Printed in Canada
First Edition 2016

Shelfie

A **free** eBook edition is available with the purchase of this print book.

CLEARLY PRINT YOUR NAME ABOVE IN UPPER CASE

Instructions to claim your free eBook edition:
1. Download the Shelfie app for Android or iOS
2. Write your name in **UPPER CASE** above
3. Use the Shelfie app to submit a photo
4. Download your eBook to any device

Contents

Dedication

Every writer should have an invisible audience. I wondered for years who would be the people reading what I write. Would I write to the people in Medellín, Colombia? To my old friends in the States? To my parents? To the leaders in Colombia with broken dreams that can still fly? To college kids bursting with life? To my old classmates in poetry class at the University of Virginia? To my old professors at Yale whom I still want to please? To you? Well, yes, in a way but not directly. I decided to write to my two sons, Andrew and Christian. I feel them looking over my shoulders. Of course, they are not literally looking at what I write now. They couldn't care less, but they will one day read this book in which I tried to hold down on paper my trembling life long enough to feel its flame. You are welcome to overhear me talking to my sons.

So, my beloved sons, I dedicate this book to you, men of purer hearts and greater dreams than I ever had.

Desire

I want to be my sons' hero,
My wife's rescuer,
A writer of poems carefully stored
In kind hearts.

I want to be a catcher of great fish,
A close friend to a few men,
And most of all,
A man conquered by the
Love of Jesus,
The only scarred one in heaven.
I want always to have a heart that craves
For things bigger than my hands can hold.
I want to be strong and content in aging
Like the sea growing dark over deep waters.
I want to be a good son to the Father.
I want to love living so much
That going to bed is always hard.
I want to hand the city of Medellín
To Jesus as a gift
And then be happy alone
With a cup of coffee
Writing a few lines
To bring to you His beauty & kindness
The way a thin line pulls
A great marlin from the deep.

Preface

The Man with Blue Sky in His Glasses

It was a spring day so beautiful it almost hurt. In fact, it did. The dogwoods were in full bloom, exams were over and I walked under the blue sky on the campus of the University of Virginia totally depressed. The white columns were bright as shirts. The spring grass and the robins singing sweetened the lawn. Outside everything was stunningly beautiful. Inside it was acidic and grey. The contrast seemed cruel. I was twisted with insecurity, heartbreaks, and a barb-wired sadness tight around my heart. If I had a clear reason for this sadness, it would have been easier, but I didn't. I was young and healthy with a bright future, but depression had settled like fog. I was a danger to myself.

And then I saw him on the other side of the street. Though he was almost fifty, his beard was still black. He was squinting through glasses that were glazed with the blue sky. He seemed content standing in front of his little church with his arms crossed and his head tilted as if to listen. I knew he was the pastor, but I wanted nothing to do with him: I had discarded Christianity. How could any intelligent person simply accept the religion of his parents or culture? I had majored in comparative religions, searching for a trace of God running through all beliefs. I had looked for a trace of God in the professors' faces. Though I was searching, I resented anyone who said they had found anything. I believed this man, smug in his Christianity, certainly could not bring any real answers or comfort to my raw heart. Yet, the day's beauty seemed to be inside him and the whole blue sky seemed to be in his glasses. It was as if I were seeing blue for the first time. I almost crossed the street to ask him about life, but he saw me looking at him and smiled. I pressed on as if in a blizzard in the midst of dogwood flowers and sunlight.

I wonder what he would have told me if I had crossed the street. What would he have told me about God? Somehow I knew this man would not disdain my questions, unlike my professor of Buddhism. He would not roll his eyes as my pot partners did when I asked the big questions about life. Somehow I knew this man was linked to the kindness of Christ, but I didn't cross over. How could the God of creation abide in a little man with his arms folded and his glasses flaming with the blue of heaven?

Four years later, Jesus Christ hounded me and captured my heart in the desert of Arizona. To say I became a Christian is to say I began an ongoing conversation with the Resurrected One.

This book is like the man standing on the other side of the street. After years of having a lovers' quarrel with Jesus and being broken, busted and forgiven, the beauty of the day is finally on the inside of me too. I still have my grey, muddled days, but the blue always wins. I will tell you what I have experienced of God and what I wish I would have known years ago. I will tell you what I don't know because I don't "have Him" anymore than the open sails have the wind. I wish I had crossed the street that day. I tracked down the man with blue sky in his glasses forty years later. It was an interesting conversation; I will save that for the end. For now, I wonder how I could talk about how the blue of heaven has invaded my life for forty years without sounding like a religious nut.

Biographies map out what happens on the surface of life, but a spiritual biography is more like a map of a sea which shows the depths, the reefs and the currents. Much of what happens on the surface is a result of what goes on underneath; at the core of everything is God who seems drunk with love for us. This book, hopefully, is a map of that deep blue sea.

I read that non-fiction and religious books lead the Kindle sales, but they are very separate categories. Non-fiction implies no nonsense, the non-miraculous. In the serious non-fiction section, we shouldn't expect God to break through the daily-ness of life. On the other hand, I recoil from the word *religious* because it suggests the boringly predictable. So, does that leave me to write irreligious non-fiction? I would like to suggest a new category: the miraculous reality. I have seen cracks in the boring routine of reality. Honest to God miracles have happened right under my nose. There is light brighter than the sun ready to break out on the dullest of days. There is a quiet voice louder than the constant noise of cities. There is a joy underneath the heaviest sorrows. There are people who smell like heaven. And there is a God who is able and willing to break into our life.

So, whether you are tired of Christians or a tired Christian, we all hunger for something more, above the day-to-day and deep beneath the night-to-night. Wouldn't it be great if there was a God who was a very good father who would talk to and touch us?

Introduction

Biographies of the Heart

You would think God would have more on His plate than hunting down some insecure, depressed and broken-hearted kid, but He is the Hound of Heaven, the Great Fisherman. At times I feel that God is like the Old Man of the sea and we are the marlin. He is always over our shoulders, pulling, giving slack, but never letting go. Jesus' promise, "I will never leave you nor forsake you," seems at times more like a threat than a promise. But it is a promise. His love is relentless, ruthless and dangerous because it will take you where you did not want to go, to love people you did not want to know and to see things you never thought existed.

I was hurled into this ministry of preaching to thousands every week, taping TV programs, overseeing churches, training leaders, teaching in conferences and dealing with lots of problems. Several times the pressure of the ministry has knocked the wind out of me. Even worse, I felt I was losing my heart. I knew I had to write. I thought I was going to be a poet, live in the mountains, fish, write books. I would smoke a pipe and have a gentle wife, happy kids, a fat dog and be mildly famous. When I was twenty-three, Christ invaded my personal space and I knew I had boarded a ship bigger than I could steer. I had received a coin with two sides: one side was the call to be His, the other was the call to pastor. I knew it instantly, but I still dreamed of a smaller life. Instead, I am married to a hard-headed woman from New Jersey, pastoring a church of thousands in a city of millions in Medellín, Colombia, and my poetry is packed away like money from another country. I once read a poem to my pastoral team that left them laughing and gasping for air—I told them no more pearls for swine. I do have a grouchy dog, two wonderful sons and a beautiful wife who won't let me smoke a pipe.

Though I was educated beyond my intelligence and I'm leading a church beyond my leadership skills, the Holy Spirit is leading me into a peace stronger than storms. Often I think my personality was made for the secluded cabin full of books and art, but I am stepping out into my deeper calling where love is not safe, peace is not storm-free and the ocean is full of sharks.

Why would anyone think his or her life is such a big deal to warrant an autobiography? A biography (*bio*: life & *graphy*: writing) is a life written down by another, but why write your own? Henry David Thoreau, the famous American poet and essayist wrote, "Life was a poem I could have lived, but I could not both live and utter it." But he took time to utter it, and strangely, his utterings about his life around Walden Pond emboldened me to live with my eyes wide open and heart pounding. I think taking time to utter our life on paper helps focus and intensify life, and perhaps enlivens others. Though I now consider Thoreau's transcendental philosophy to be romantic mush, I am indebted to the man for stirring my heart in high school to live for something higher than getting a job, retiring, dying and having a funeral where everybody eats potato salad and goes home.

I think, outside of the Bible, nothing ennobles and enlightens us like a good biography. Getting the feel of an entire life within a week of reading helps us to see the big brush strokes of life. When you measure your life by decades instead of days, you almost hear the background music of a great epic. You are not just facing mundane problems in a boring life, but you are the hero of a great movie.

A biography also helps us to feel the importance of our ordinary struggles.

If we overcome depression, a bad attitude or the fear of confrontation, we are really winning a battle for others, too. Our little victory could be a great victory for people around us and for our children. On the other hand, our little yielding to temptation, anger or depression may have serious consequences for everyone in our area of influence. A biography opens the eyes to see that our carnal problems are really struggles of eternal importance. Instead of just getting through hassles complaining, "Why do I have to put up with this crap?" we sense that hassles are heroic opportunities. Instead of the daily difficulties wearing us down, we gain an inner strength facing the challenges.

The best biographies are the ones that deal with the dance between the inner life and the outer quests. An autobiography by a politician who is still running is boring. He is editing his inner life, dodging his fears and failures. We want to hear about when he went through hell. We want to hear about the unseen victory in the heart that was like a colorful banner, giving him courage to win the outward battle.

Writing this book required some time alone and silence from the thousand voices in the ministry. It was hard leaving the church in Colombia for two months, but I found out that my busy schedule is not so important and that the church needed a break from me. I told my friends I was heading to the mountains like Jeremiah Johnson to fight the wild Indians of my soul.

Here in Florida, I am writing from a cluttered soul with strange longings and recurrent thoughts needing to be unwound and sorted out. It is like going through a drawer full of old letters, gifts, coins from another country, broken watches and telephone numbers of people I don't remember. Do the letters still speak? Should I keep the gifts? Is there any country where the coins are still of value? Do the watches tell me what time it is? Do the numbers still connect? I need to pour the whole drawer out on the floor and pick up each item in the light of my calling. Somehow thoughts get untangled when they pass through your fingers onto paper.

Sometimes writing is like taking time to get some knots out of my fishing line in order to cast long and deep again. And sometimes writing is like trying to catch wild birds and then setting them loose inside a great hall where they spiral upwards, singing around the columns. In these pages, I try to catch the wildest yearnings that race in the heart and set them free on white pages. I know these birds cannot be kept inside. There is something about confining their thousand-mile range into a few wide circles inside a book that helps us appreciate their beauty and grace. In the same way, you cannot live inside books and ideas, but they can inspire you to see greater and rise higher. We are crazy to believe that we can catch a little of eternity in our hearts, but God has made us a little bit crazy.

Since my conversion, I have been a walking contradiction: studying at Yale, speaking in tongues in a Cajun church, coaching in a private school and preaching Spanish with a West Virginia accent. At times I want to quit the ministry, hide from people and train a big dog to bite anyone who comes near me with a big Bible. Yet His presence has been the constant through the years. Somehow the membrane between heaven and earth grows thinner and the surprise of the supernatural seems to be increasing with time.

I will tell you some supernatural stories, but I will not leave out the hurts and doubts. When Peter pulled on the net filled with miracle fish, there was probably some rotting seaweed in there, too. Seaweed is everywhere in this book. Miracles are increasing, but my control of them is not. I seem to find myself needing them to happen more and more. Somehow life is not easier, but better.

Since I thought I was going to be a poet, and still yearn for the peace of a writing desk and a life of unhurried conversations, I'll start you on this journey with a poem I wrote on an unhurried day off:

A Day Off

I thank the night for letting this morning go
The city wakes so bright and slow,
Cars crash the air like breakers down the shore

And dishes rattle in the house next door.
Praise Him for letting this morning go.

No one to call, no one to see,
A dog digs an ear into ecstasy.
The sun makes me simple and free
One day to spend on me.
The sun breaks out of the star-kissed sea.
Praise Him for letting this morning go.

PART ONE

WAKING UP ON FIRE

We are fired into life with a certain madness...
We do not wake up in this world calm and serene...
We wake up crying, on fire, with desire, with madness.
What we do with this desire is our spirituality.

—FATHER RONALD ROLHEISER

The Holy Longing

ONE

Fishing and Great Expectations

I woke up on fire in West Virginia on June 21, 1952, in the McMillan hospital, which my grandfather founded. Sometimes I think I remember being born in a dim hospital room filled with people making a fuss. It may just be a memory of an imagination, but it is a fact that June 21 was the first day of summer, announcing freedom from school for millions of kids all over the United States. The July 2, 1952 Daily Mail reads:

We would like to welcome a newcomer to Charleston who has a much loved name…William Andrew McMillan, new son of Thomas Harvey and Charlotte McMillan, much to the delight of his parents and his sister, Mardi. He already is being called "W. A." as his doctor granddaddy was before him.

My grandfather, Dr. Mac, died a year before I was born, but his portrait in the hospital's reception room pulsed with life that seemed to say to me, "Now you do it." He was a big, portly man with a suit, vest, gold watch chain, soft round face and bifocals; I always took my name seriously. Shortly after my conversion, I was rummaging through the old documents in the Kanawha Presbyterian Church, where he dozed off for more than fifty years. I found the church's 1950 yearbook, just before his death. It contained a short biography of each member and their favorite Bible verses. My grandfather chose,

> *Let not your heart be troubled: ye believe in God, believe also in me. In my Father's house are many mansions: if it were not so, I would have told you. I go to prepare a place for you.*
>
> JOHN 14:1–2 KJV

He must have liked the personal guarantee.

I went to a Sunday school right across the street, where it seemed everyone was intent on putting out my fire. I came home one day almost in tears. As my Mom told it, I said, "All they talk about there is Jesus, Jesus, Jesus." I hated being cooped up inside a dark room listening to stories about a man in a bathrobe carrying lambs around. I wanted to climb trees and throw rocks at hornet's nests. For me, Summer Bible School was as close to hell as I wanted to get. But if we read the Bible for ourselves, we will see that Jesus is anything but boring. When the followers of Jesus went to the tomb, they did not find a Bible and a note from Jesus saying, "Good luck." They found an empty tomb. They heard a woman's rumor about Jesus being alive and wanting to see them. They were skeptics, as are all jilted romantics. I bet they were sarcastic, too. On the way to the grave, Peter might have said, "Sure, Jesus will be there and tell us to change the world. Yea, that will happen." But something exciting and supernatural happened to change these frightened grown-ups into men with a lion in their chests. Something that called to the fire inside of them. This was adventure. This was what my heart longed for. Why didn't anyone tell me?

(I did have an exciting experience in Sunday school when I stuck a copper wire into the electrical outlet. The power sleeping in the wall bit me like snake and old Miss Sadie screamed.)

Having the self-control of a ferret did not make it any easier.

When I was thirteen, I went to the Presbyterian's youth gathering with the plan to endure the forty-five-minute meeting and then take off to meet some girls a few blocks away, but the youth leader kept us squirming on the couch for almost two hours. I hated church and I hated this guy talking about the Bible. I wanted life, the night air and the girls. There was no connection between Jesus Christ and the thrill of the night, the life tingling in my veins and the girls, girls, girls! Maybe the youth leader was trying to tell me something about the fire and maybe he was a burning bush. But church folk sure make it hard to see that.

Everyone hungers for the thrill of love and transcendent experiences. The heart demands it. We don't want circus miracles that just amaze us; we can't take the circus home. Often miracles we hear about are just a nice show for somebody else. Often the miracles on TV with big hair evangelists seem unnatural and mystical, like a tornado full of fire but never touching the ground where we live. We yearn for that sweet part of the bat where the supernatural stirs our dust and leaves us different. We ache for signs that there is a personal beautiful God behind the stars who is gazing at us and coming closer than the light in our eyes. We are crazy with the hope of living and loving forever.

I think God speared us in the heart with eternity. That is why we feel pain when we see the red sun setting over the mountains. It is beautiful but it aches, too. That is why we ache hearing the long cry of Canadian geese flying over continents. We desire more than this world can give. We yearn for eternity in the small cup of seventy years. We ache for beauty that would kill us if we could see it. And yet we can easily ignore this wound of eternity, and sell out to saner things like real estate, a good salary, cruises and fine dining, or to the basic pulls of drugs, lusts and violence, because the heart must beat for something. We become like the thousand-mile geese who settle for dirty cow ponds. But we are not made for this filthy comfort; we know there is more to life than hard work, taxes, death and the funeral with everyone eating potato salad and going home.

Once they asked Mohammad Ali what he really wanted from life. He said, "I just want to live forever." Where do we get a desire like that? We even want more; we dare to dream of such things like being in love and being loved forever. I think eternal life must exist because the human heart demands it. Why would God wake us up on fire if He did not plan to give us eternity? Jesus said He left earth to build our eternal dwellings. Then He said, "If it weren't so, I wouldn't have told you." Either God is super cruel or crazy good. Does God make us ache for eternity only to yank the rug from under our feet? Does He give us an eternal personhood exploding with love to just throw us away? Again, Jesus tells us that beyond what we can see, there are some wonderful dwellings places. If it were not so, He would not have raised our expectation (see John 14:1–4).

You may or may not be a Christian, but you ought to know that Christ has not come to corral your heart into small doctrines and small desires. He has come to wake you to your greater desires. He has come to make you insecure with your securities and unsatisfied with your satisfaction. His spear is aimed at your heart. He wants to take you out of the cow pond and into the blue sky. He calls you to paint your life with all the colors on the palette and beyond. Your life is not an essay to read, but a song to sing.

When I took the confirmation class of the Presbyterian Church, I told the pastor I was not sure if I believed in Christ. I did not have a clue what it meant that He died for me on a cross. It was like hearing about a man shooting himself in Cambodia and hearing he did it for you. He told me to go ahead with the confirmation and that I would believe in it all later. It was probably not the right answer, but he was right—I would believe it all.

My teenage summers were spent driving a winding road to the country club in a yellow convertible, looking for girls at bars and trying to make something funny happen, usually with the help of alcohol. We partied with various drugs, beer, booze and even Freon (the gas used in refrigerators.) Janice Joplin crooned on the radio,

"It's summertime and the livin' is easy." I lived with a broken heart and I was on a quest to find the right girl. I was also on a quest to do things just for the sake of experience, like stealing the coonskin hat off the West Virginian mascot during a football game against Virginia.

I did not have any goals or dreams and thought becoming an adult was something you put off as long as possible. Most of my friends knew what they wanted to do, but I wondered what I wanted to be. If a friend told me he wanted to take over his father's business, I wondered why and what it had to do with life and death. The older I grew the more I thought about the big reasons for living. A job and making money were not enough. I would ask friends why they wanted a job and a home when it all ends with a funeral and potato salad. I thought the answers must be hidden in philosophy, poetry, psychology, or religion. I discarded Christianity because the big issues of life and death were never covered in my Presbyterian Sunday School.

The first time I remember praying to God—not just thinking about Him—was at a dance at a country club. I had drunk vodka mixed with beer and was throwing my guts up in the parking lot. I was thirteen and knew I had lost my bet with my Dad, who had offered me $2,000 if I didn't smoke or drink until I was twenty-one. I was feeling so lousy that I looked up to the stars and promised God I would never drink again if He'd rescue me from the agony. Though I got drunk a week later, it was the first time I remember really talking to God. And God was there, but just there, silent and impersonal.

Praying is like fishing. You cast into the sea and wait. Your line sinks into the invisible blue. After a while you are as sleepy as the sea gull glinting in the sun's glare and the slow swells. It seems there is nothing in the deep blue dark. It seems nothing will ever change. Suddenly, a tug. Something alive taps your line. Then it jerks and your reel bursts on fire. Your line stretches out and springs from the water, flaming with the colors of the rainbow. Your heart is alive, fastened to the invisible, to something bigger than you. It is huge, frightened and fighting for its life, and in a way you are fighting for life, too. Life connects to life. The visible is connected to the invisible and you are more alive than ever.

If this happens hooking up to a bull shark, what happens when God tugs? Your heart sings and bursts into flames. I can attest to the tugs of God on my little life. I have been skunked on many fishing trips, yawned through many dog-day afternoons and felt as if nothing really was going to change. Then the line clicks, pulls hard and I am connected with the invisible.

Hattie, our maid, would sit at the kitchen table, eating and telling me how people would cry at the altar in her church and feel God like fire. She told me she was born again. I thought how great it could be if I could start all over again, but never dreamed that it was possible for me. Somehow I thought that clean slates and second chances were for other people. Maybe it was just for people like Hattie. Besides her, I'd never heard of anyone having an encounter with Christ until I was about seventeen, when Danny Gandy, the meanest kid in town who had previously beat my friend John to a pulp, told us he was born again. I thought God had a lot of nerve to help the biggest jerk in town. I can still remember drinking root beer with a few friends and coming to the conclusion it was impossible for a jerk to be made into another person. Danny Gandy would be a jerk forever. The only difference was he was now a religious jerk.

God seemed to me as the distant wizard of Oz, who didn't care when I was vomiting between the cars and feeling sorry for myself at the bar.

Then more tugs. My conscience wouldn't let me rest. I hated the feelings of guilt from lying and sexual sins. I felt a little guilty for stealing liquor from my Dad. He had the storage room filled with eight boxes of whiskey. My sister and I thought he would miss the liquor if we stole a few bottles, but if we stole a whole box, he'd never miss it. When I was arrested for drinking at fourteen, my Dad picked me up at the police station. I was more afraid of his face than of the police.

Before the judge a week later, my Dad said, "Judge, he is a good boy." I remember thinking, "I wish I were." The guilt was gnawing from deep inside. Something was tugging.

Mostly, my life then felt like a long afternoon where nothing would ever change; nights in bars feeling lonely and sorry for myself, thinking it was all about luck and I didn't have any. I was caught in the lie of self-pity and bad luck.

Paul thought life was pretty boring too, just one thing after another, until Jesus busted his reality. After his encounter with Him on the Damascus road, Paul lived on the pins and needles of expectation. He sensed all of creation groaning with this expectation, too. He wrote in Romans 8:19, "For the earnest expectation of the creation waits for the manifestation of the sons of God." (KJV 2000) If you read quickly through the whole New Testament, you sense there is a huge wave about to crash over everything. And over the years this expectation is increasing.

It is amazing how one long hot afternoon lures us into sameness, into thinking that life will never really change. Then the wind comes and startles us. Where was this wind birthed; over a fast river or a colorful forest? Where will it go and will it become so weak that it can't even lift the lock on a girl's forehead? There is another wind. It comes from heaven and it tells me things really can change and it will change me more than my body can bear. There is a wind that my skin cannot feel. Years ago I wrote this poem:

About
When the thunder is about to break,
The clouds about to rain,
And the wind about to lift
The tender white underbellies of the leaves
And we know we are about to become bright like angels

When the wave seems to suspend
Before breaking on the sand

Like a thousand men throwing
Their wine glasses against the hearth,

What is holding us
From the crazed celebration of
Flames, praising in the wind,
And all of us running home forever?

*

You could hardly tell of any urgency
When you see the tractor tilling the land
For the spring planting,
The mountain shadows take
Hours to cover the fields,
And tourists in the old bookstore
Move as slow as the tides.

But looking again,
The small spring leaves beat like the hearts
Of frightened animals.
The sparrows can hardly stay on a branch
For more than a few seconds.
The trout twitch suddenly in the streams.
They cannot keep the secret for much longer.
The fox's eyes stare
At the door about to open
He is about to step out
From the wet stars.

Once in Colombia, at one of our church meetings in the bullring, I prayed for a woman who was blind. I was tired and just wanted to go home. I had never seen a blind person healed. I had heard about them but had never seen it happen. When I prayed for her she fell down. When they helped her up she looked dizzy in more ways than one. I prayed for her again and she fell down screaming. I thought I had hurt her. But she started screaming that she could see. I doubted her story, so I asked her two friends who came with her. They assured me she had been blind, and they were tired of taking care of her. Imagine how it was for her to have light and bright images rush into her darkness like a dam breaking. The question is simple: Do you believe that you could hear things and see things that you have never imagined, or do you think that the rest of your life will only be a boring repetition of all you have seen and heard? Paul said,

Ear has not heard, nor eye has seen nor has the imagination conceived what God has prepared for those they love Him....but the Spirit has revealed them to us.

1 CORINTHIANS 2:9–10 *(Author's paraphrase)*

There is something wonderful about a sense of expectation where anything can change. It is a gift. After dinner in a restaurant in Guatemala, the waiter served coffee to everyone but me. Then he left the room and I felt slighted. He served coffee to my eight friends, but seemed to ignore me intentionally. I wondered if I had done something to offend him. If anyone needed coffee it was me because I was addicted to coffee, and this waiter walks off without looking in my direction. It was hard not to take it personally. Strange how many hurts seem to resurface in a small offense. When he returned, I asked him to fill my cup and he said, "Señor, I thought you did not want coffee. Everyone had their coffee cup with the face up—*la boca hacia arriba*—but you had your cup with the face down—*la boca hacia abajo.*"

So often we think God should be moved by our need, but it should be obvious to us by now that being needy does not move God. We try to build a case with God how much our needs make us deserve more, but nothing happens. We feel hurt and wonder why God is dealing out His blessings to other people, leaving us high and dry. We take unanswered prayers personally and wonder what God has against us.

Jesus, however, teaches that God is not moved by need but by faith. And faith is having the cup facing up with expectation.

The Bible also teaches that God is a good Father, who "gives good gifts to those to ask Him," (Matthew 7:11). To live with expectation; we have to know there is something to expect. We have to know the nature of the One who gives. How often we enter into a prayer time or into a worship service with the cup of our heart facedown. We have no expectation that God will speak or touch us. We only have our secret arguments about why God should bless us, but our hearts are turned upside down. Isaiah 30:18 says, "So the LORD must wait for you to come to him so he can show you his love and compassion. For the LORD is a faithful God. Blessed are those who wait for his help." (NLT)

God is pouring out His Spirit in abundance and we have our cups turned down and are upset. Sometimes our cup has been upside down for so long that it is stuck to the saucer.

Jesus did not make a case study of each person. He did not scan a person to see how much he deserved or needed the miracle. He just said things like, "Don't be afraid; just believe." "All things are possible for those who believe." "According your faith, be it done to you." We could argue with Him, or we could just turn the cup up. Expectation opens the heavens above our little life. I could have complained about the waiter or quietly resented him, but I turned my cup over and got my coffee. What if I lived and prayed with my heart face up?

Maybe your cup has never faced up but you know now is the time. There is something, someone, tugging at your heart. I have seen countless people make the decision to say yes to Jesus, and God always fills those cups.

TWO

West Virginia

A human life, I think, should be well-rooted in some spot of a native land, where it may get the love of tender kinship for the face of the earth, for the labors men go forth to, for the sounds and accents that haunt it, for whatever will give that early home a familiar unmistakable difference amidst the future widening of knowledge. The best introduction to astronomy is to think of the nightly heavens as a little lot of stars belonging to one's own homestead.

—GEORGE ELIOT

We love the smell of the dirt of our homeland, especially West Virginians. Now I know our state is about last in the country in education, economy and health care, but it is first in obesity and toothless grins. We don't love our kids because they are on the honor roll. We love them because they get along with people and get over things quickly. We love our State. The quote above by George Eliot introduces the movie, *Gettysburg*, suggesting that Robert E Lee chose to fight for the South because of his roots in Virginia. Despite his love for the Union and his aversion to slavery, his devotion to his homeland owned him.

I rooted for all the Mountaineers teams even when I attended the University of Virginia and Yale. Though I have lived in South America for more than a quarter of a century, West Virginian news is still local news to me. Every time I fly back to the mountains, the twang of the stewardess welcoming me to Charleston reminds me how deep is the goodness of the people. There is a sweetness in the Scotch-Irish culture preserved by the mountains over the last three centuries. The patch of stars there are kinder.

The people of Medellín, Colombia, where I live now, passionately love their city, but more with a fierce pride than those of West Virginia. When I first came to Medellín, the taxi cab driver boasted Medellín had the best soccer players, the best businessmen, the best beauty queens and a mafia known all over the world. The people of Medellín have a certain push, or initiative, unmatched in Colombia. One Paisa (slang for someone who lives in Medellín) told me that you never need to ask a Paisa where he is from: if he is from Medellín, he will tell you. If he's not from Medellín, why embarrass him? Now, I am a two-timing scoundrel; I love the kindness of West Virginia, and I have that fierce Paisa pride. Heaven will be a mixture of the two.

Growing up, I remember playing outdoors and feeling life was kind and blue like the sky. The only enemies were the big bumblebees buzzing around us. But one summer day we were playing inside the home of a friend when suddenly the grown-ups filled the kitchen and ambulance sirens accentuated the fear on their faces. Only years later did I learn what really happened. A mother accidently backed over her son in front of the house. In her panic she lurched the car forward and ran over him again. The child died instantly. I did not know what was happening, but I knew it was bigger than grown-ups. I somehow knew my safe world could be invaded by something that was not meant to be. One minute I was playing with toy cars on the floor, and the next minute the air could be gashed open by evil.

Do you remember when the blue was not broken? For many the blue sky was broken by sexual abuse, domestic violence or by just dad falling drunk on the kitchen floor.

Maybe you remember your parents screaming and slamming doors or the lights of an ambulance turning the side of the house red and blue. The problem is that as we age, we think it normal to accept that this world is not right. I think Jesus comes to awaken the heart to feel again—to shake us out of accepting the status quo of brokenness and tragedy and to show us we can pray for His Kingdom to come to earth as it is in Heaven. Jesus came to help us remember that we once believed that everything should be right; He came to help us believe it can be right again.

Right after Jesus talked about the hardness of heart that causes divorce (Matthew 18), He called the children. He did not want to tell them about why their sky was broken. He just wanted to hold them and bless them. I bet those kids remembered that. While the grown-ups were arguing over the doctrine of marriage and divorce, the kids were deep in the arms of Jesus. They were absorbing the doctrine of "what was and will one day be."

The Mystery Hole

When I was nine years old my Dad bought a vacation farm in Organ Cave, three long hours from home. Halfway between Charleston and Organ Cave glimmers an opening to another dimension. A hand painted sign on the side of the road, in letters dripping with terror, said, *Mystery Hole: One Dollar.* My sister and I begged our parents to stop every time we passed it, but they never stopped. My father always tried to beat his record for the trip, and of course had no idea why it was important to do so. We men have small stadiums in our heads pushing us to win invisible races. We would stop at *Paradise Inn*, a small restaurant run by two old sisters who never smiled. My Dad called them the Gold Dust Twins and would greet them with a big, "So glad to see you two beautiful gals," but they never undid their frown. So, *Paradise*, yes, but *the Mystery Hole*, never.

We wondered what was in the hole. Why couldn't our parents see the importance of exploring a possible crack in reality? Maybe it was purple smoke that formed into a face that would tell us something deep about life. Or there were colors we have never seen and fragrances we have never dreamed of smelling. Or just an alien chained to a post. We could not imagine the mystery hole.

Professors write off our desire for the mysterious as an ancient urge to explain thunder, and now that we know about electricity, the desire is obsolete. I think thunder only reminds us of the greater unknown. The Bible says God put eternity in our hearts. Just being alive in this endless universe is unexplainable. We know there is mystery and as kids we want to stop and look for it, but as we get older, we step on the gas.

Years later, my sister and I got off the Interstate to travel the old Route 60 and finally stopped at the Mystery Hole. An old lady with brown teeth took our dollar and told us to enjoy the hole. We walked across a small bridge with moving planks that entered into the room full of mirrors, distorted and curved. Then we passed through a small dark tunnel with red demon faces lighting up on both sides. The whole trip took about 45 seconds and ended in the souvenir shop with Mystery Hole coffee cups, aprons and T-shirts. We laughed so hard the old lady thought we were high. All those years of wondering and now the mystery was revealed. We told our parents we experienced the Mystery Hole, but we were sworn to secrecy. Now they wanted to know.

Most of the mysterious holes have been explained and we are too smart to be suckered into mystery merchants. Moses' life had been one long disappointment. He tried to do something great for Israel and failed. Now forty years of routine pastoring had dulled his expectation for anything to change. He was walking by a bush on fire, but there was the kid in him screaming to stop. So the text says he stopped to look at the bush. And two things happened. First, he noticed that the bush burned and burned, but did not burn up. He would have never noticed if he had not stopped. Secondly, when God saw him looking, He spoke to him by name. That is important—only after he stopped did God speak. How many burning bushes have we passed? How many times was God about to speak to us, but we sped on?

Usually God won't use a sign you can read as clear as the *Mystery Bush* one. The signs are easy to miss if you don't stop and pay attention. The sky might look so strange coming home. You may notice the same word appearing several times during the day. You may remember a dream late in the day when you see a bird land on a snowy fence. Under a butter-colored lamp, one verse in the Bible strangely warms your heart, and you look around the empty house and feel it is the first time in years that you have stopped to look.

The fire in the little bush became the fire on the mountain and the fire in the night sky over the Israelites. When I have paid attention to mystery signs and stopped to look, the signs became turning points. One night when I was drunk, I read about Jesus being the light to every man. It was such a small glimmer, but I paid attention and now my whole life is washed with the light of Jesus. He is pretty much what I live for and do.

Another day, I saw this girl sitting at a table. I went back to my office that night and said out loud to God, "I think I just met my wife." Six years later we were married.

I did not know where Colombia was on the map, but the first time I really heard "Colombia" a fire that had been burning in me all my life flared up. I used to have a big birthmark that looked like South America backwards on my chest, and within the birthmark right where Colombia should be, I had a darker mark. It has disappeared, or rather, sunk deep into my heart. I think when God calls us to a place, the place has been already there inside us from birth.

The Bible calls miracles *signs* because they point to something much greater. A sign that says, *Nashville: 40 miles* is just a piece of metal pointing us to a city full of lights, life and music. We are not supposed to gawk at the sign, but move toward the city. Miracles are just signs pointing us to a city where the lights never go off. Signs get us moving again, loving again, trusting again. I believe just reading this book will prep the atmosphere around you to feel the tug of God.

I hope as you read you will feel a growing sense that something huge is swirling underneath, inside and above you. Maybe my story is just the sign you need, right now.

But it takes faith to pay attention, to stop when a sign pops up. Faith like a child. We must listen to that childlike desire in us to see God's greatness in order to not pass by that burning bush.

Punched out Faith

I was thumbing for a ride in Virginia Beach once, when a car full of sailors stopped. I ran up to the car and they took off. So I mentioned something about their mother and they stopped again. I was seventeen and believed the best in everyone, assured they wouldn't hit me. But the first one out of the car punched me in the left cheek. I went down and got up. He slugged me again in the exact same place, and I went down in the exact same place. Another sailor offered to help me up, but I said I'd rather not. They laughed and took off. An hour later, I had a blue cantaloupe on the left side of my face. Sometimes we'd rather stay down than risk getting knocked down again. We'd rather pass by the burning bush than risk stopping and not hearing anything.

(Many years later, I had a root canal. The dentist asked if I'd ever been hit in the left cheek. When I told him the story, he said that probably caused the nerve damage. I never knew a punch could hit you from a distance of thirty years away.)

Thomas wasn't at the meeting when Jesus appeared to the disciples after dying on the Cross. The disciples were excited and wanted to give Thomas a heads up. He wanted to believe that Jesus was alive, but could not take another punch like seeing Jesus naked and nailed to the Cross. Thomas thought it better not to believe; better to keep your faith on the floor.

Most atheists are disappointed romantics. If you dig into the history of those who mock God, you will find a tragedy, or a sucker punch. We all have some hurts that hurt like root canal, hurting more deeply over time. Maybe you lost a child. Maybe you've experienced the pain of betrayal. But like our wounds of the past can overcome us, the wounds of Jesus can come to heal us.

When I was eight years old, at Virginia Beach again, the rip tide pulled me under. My mother saw me go, but there was nothing she could do. I still remember being tossed around like in a washing machine, not knowing where the surface was. Suddenly, a wave pulled me out and threw me on the beach. It was a rogue wave, larger than the rest. I once read an article saying that waves are formed on one side of the Atlantic and will travel eight days to the east coast, keeping their form and surge. I believe God formed the rogue wave eight days before, sending it at the right time to lift and spit me on the beach. In the same way, what Jesus did 2000 years before has been rolling toward us and will hit us right where we need it. If you risk having faith, you may get disappointed again. You may get hurt. You might even deserve it, like I did. But you will be lifted up again to dream and love, thanks to His wounds.

The only hand that could lift Thomas up would be the hand with the wound. The disciples had been in the same frame of mind a week earlier when Jesus appeared to them and said, "Peace." They were too shell-shocked to receive peace; so Jesus had to show them His scars so that they could receive the peace. Thomas had to see the scars. Maybe we would do better to show our scars, too.

Jesus died for us and came back to show his scars to those who needed peace and faith. We can trust Him with our wound and then we can walk away from them hand in hand with Jesus. He still stands today, ready to show you the scars from the Cross. The scars that brought us life and healing. He is safe. He is our way out. People are tired of big-haired, grinning Christians. Only the wounded are healers.

THREE

Homesick

I was the most homesick kid at Wallawhatoola (Indian name for Winding Waters). Maybe most of the kids at summer camp listened to the rain tap the tent roof with pools of water in their eyes, yearning for home, but I was the worst. I was nine years old, and six weeks were forever. When I was thirteen years old, I remember watching my parents drive away from the boarding school in Virginia, my home for the next four years. I would have felt better if someone had punched me in the solar plexus. I knew I would never live at home again, though I would visit for holidays and summers. From there I went to college at the University of Virginia, traveled west, built bridges in Wyoming, taught school and coached in Arizona and New Orleans. Then after graduating from Yale Divinity School in Connecticut, I pastored for six years in New Jersey. Suddenly, I was married and living in South America, and that has been home for the last thirty years. As a boy from the soft hills of West Virginia, Medellín, Colombia is very far from home on the map of my heart. But God burned a love for the people within me and home is where the heart burns. As the Jesuits say, the journey is my home.

I think most people feel like the homesick kid, but won't admit it. We are not at home in our strange little life. We may own our own home with double-locked doors, but homelessness seeps into the heart. Just the title of Tom Wolf's book, *You Can't Go Home*

Again, haunts us. The German poet, Rilke, said we are always saying goodbye—goodbye to the home of childhood, the home of youth, and the home of middle age. As soon as we settle into one stage of life, it changes and moves us out. Men do not feel at home in their grown-up bodies, and women are homesick for that place where someone will fight to the death to protect their beauty.

Maybe the rising compassion for the homeless today is because we, too, feel so homeless. Maybe the housing crisis is really a homeless crisis. Divorce, death, violence, abuse, foreclosures have crashed into the homes of most everyone. Safety is gone. I think God created this huge passion in us for a wonderful, cozy, loving home with cookies, sleeping dogs and patterns of sunlight on golden rugs, but as we grow older we realize that the chance of finding home in this life is slim.

I remember hitchhiking across America and walking at night by homes with butter-colored lights burning in the kitchen windows. It seemed everyone was at home but me, but I later learned how homeless most homes are. I remember the first time I drove down Main Street in the small town of Allentown, New Jersey, where I would pastor for six years. The old homes were bright white with perfect yards and hanging flowers. I thought how easy and warm each home must be. Later I got to know the pain of every one of those homes: widows, suicide, leg amputation, divorce, child drowning, adultery, bankruptcy, alcoholism and a kid on drugs. The houses seemed to be rafts drifting farther away from home. As I would pray with these families, I told them we had a decision to make: believe we are homeless, fatherless and alone, drifting farther from home, or dare to believe that we are actually on the way home.

One of the reasons that I fell in love with Jesus was because He did not have a place to rest His head. He was a hunted man. When He died homeless on the Cross, He cried out to the dark heavens, "God, why have you forsaken me?" This was not poetry. Jesus was suffering homelessness for us. He tasted eternal homelessness so that we could go home. I believe that, but I will not say I still do not feel homesick.

In some ways, I am more homesick than ever. The Bible says that God put eternity (*olam*) in our hearts. He puts a Grand Canyon in us that nothing on earth can fill. The yearning for *olam* hurts so much that we try to divert our hearts to yearn for lesser things. But when we fill our life with the best of the lesser things, like fame and wealth, we feel the hurt even more. That is why so many Hollywood stars are nuts. We walk around in a permanent state of discontentment. We know something is askew but we don't know how to fix it.

Explain the sound of geese yearning for home in the fire-red evening, and people filling churches to listen to dull sermons just for a whiff of home. As Augustine wrote, God gave us restless hearts until they find their rest in Him. This restlessness knows there must be a place where we can rest and be loved. This earth hints of this. Scientists say this planet is the target of a kind intention. There are thousands of variables, like the precise angle of the earth's axis, the perfect distance from the sun, the size and pull of the moon, etc., that keep us in this tender sphere of life. I would be impressed with an older kid spinning a basketball on his finger, but this spinning planet is amazing; and yet, we yearn for more than earth can give us.

The greatest evidence that heaven exists is that our hearts demand it. We hunger and bread exists. Our lungs yearn for air and oxygen blankets the planet. We ache for warmth and there is plenty of it from our big sun. So if our hearts ache for a place where we are sons and daughters forever, there must be a such home.

At Yale, one professor speculated that dogs probably ate the body of Jesus at Calvary, the city dump that doubled for crucifixions. On the very week of his resurrection, most people tried to explain the resurrection away, too. Some said the soldiers stole his body or the crazy women went to the wrong tomb. And now this professor brings up the "dog ate my homework" excuse. Jesus did die on the garbage heap. The last thing he smelled was rotten garbage. If anyone deserved to be enjoying home on the Passover vacation, it was Jesus. But he was homeless and naked, squirming on the Cross and turning the worst city spot into a garden.

My mom used to put the organic garbage in a small bag in the kitchen. When it was full and smelly, she would call my Dad to take the rotten bag outside. "Harvey, get rid of this stinking trash." He would take the organic mush and dump it on his little garden where tomato seeds were waiting. Then in the summer, the tomatoes would swell and brighten, becoming red and succulent. My mom would look through the window and say, "Harvey, bring in those tomatoes." Trash was transformed into something delicious and desirable. What was rejected was now welcomed into the house. The Desire of the Nations transformed the worst place, a cross, into a way home. Calvary is the place where all our trash—all the rotten things that have kept us from home—was poured out on Him. Now the Father says to the Son, "Bring my sons and daughters back inside the house," (Isaiah 43:6, Author's paraphrase).

These days I feel at home in Jupiter, Florida, near the ocean. We live in Colombia full time but I love it when the plane touches down on U.S. soil and we drive north to our resting place in Jupiter. The pastel skies and the warm, kind air embrace me. I love the peace of the writing desk, the coffee shops and the walk to the beach with three rods and a bucket. But when I worship on a dirty floor in the stuffy heat of our church in Colombia, I feel at home, too. All that I want from the trip to Florida and all that I want from walking into our apartment, putting down my suitcases and opening the doors to the evening air, is what I seek in His presence—the sense of home. Jesus says He is making us many dwelling places (John 14:2). Many. On the beach. On the floor.

Heidi Baker tells about some missionaries who built a house for families. The kids ran into a house, asking their mother, "Is this ours? Is it ours? Our place? Ours?" They never had a home before. Millions never have that experience. I remember the contrast of living in the college dorm and returning home to my own room, so peaceful and rich in the gold evening light. We yearn for our own dwelling place.

There is a peace that comes in knowing nothing on earth can fill that yearning, and in knowing it will be fulfilled in heaven. Kneeling on the stained, dirty rug in Medellín, I give up my dwelling place near the shore where the bright fish wait in the breakers. He promises He is preparing for me another place where my heart will be like a kid waking up at home to the smell of cut grass and the realization that it is the first day of a long summer.

I am reading again *You Can't Go Home Again* by Thomas Wolfe. I read it forty years ago because I was leaving home. I now am reading it because my sons are leaving home for college. At Christmas, my sons will visit home and the house will seem as a museum. They will be proud of their new world in the States but they will walk through the house with reverence. They dream about returning to Colombia to continue the work of pastoring, planting churches and raising leaders, but the direction of their homesickness will shift from the past to the future, to a girl, to a home.

The week before they left, their Colombian friends threw a surprise party for them. The older folk told stories of Andrew and Christian when they were toddlers and their friends told stories of the last few years, which seems to them pretty much their whole real life. They put together a video of pictures of Andrew and Christian from birth to the present. As we watched my sons grow nineteen years in a half hour, their buddies ridiculed them and the girls cried—a dream come true for teenage boys. In the midst of the catcalls, the ice cream and guacamole mix, we remembered all the noisy chaos of the years. The pictures awakened and sharpened memories. What a racket they made for nineteen years. Then, as the video was ending, all the clatter of their life fused into one sound of a deep river running to the sea. The waters in their hearts are deep. Lord, are they deep.

Of course, we are so proud of them. They left their ministry teams in good order and left their computers, cameras and guitars for the work of the church. They left behind the only world they knew, where they were the pastor's sons, where jokes are in Spanish and where the youth sweat when they worship. I am sure they will be homesick for the past, but also for the future.

I am not sure when my homesickness shifted from the past to the future, and even toward heaven. It may have happened suddenly, like a ship passing over the Equator and the water in the sink spirals down in the opposite direction. Or it may have happened slowly, like aging. I only know that when Kathy and I left our sons in the hills of Tennessee to head back to Colombia, the knife of homesickness cut deep. It was not depressing. The pain was rich and good. I was grateful that God lets us love so deeply. The last days we spent with our boys opened our hearts to the beauty of home and to our homesickness for the future. Jesus said "In my Father's house are many *mansions* and I go to prepare a home for you" (John 14:2, author's paraphrase). There really is a heaven more real than the chair you are sitting on, where we will completely wake up. We will see for the first time a place we have always known to be, where the bright goodness of God is like a summer day that will never end, and not one bit of darkness can remain, not even in the heart. In the same chapter, Jesus says, "If a man loves me, he will keep my word, and my Father will love him, and we will make our *home* with him" (John 14:23). The word for *home* (*mone*) here is the same word in verse 2 for *mansions*. These are the only two times in the Bible where this word is found. Perhaps it does not mean white-pillared *mansions*, but it does mean a place, a home, where you will want to stay forever. It means our hearts can be mansions in the now when we love and listen to Jesus.

The day I watched my parents drive away from me at Virginia Episcopal School, I didn't know my mother was bawling. I was too busy mustering all my strength not to cry. I had to turn and face a school of boys I didn't know. My new roommate from Culpepper, Virginia, threw my clothes on the floor and then sucker punched me in the nose. I walked to the dining hall biting my lip, trying not to cry.

It got better over the four years, but it was never home. I am grateful for the discipline, the academics and the good teachers who taught me how to love learning. I am especially grateful for my Latin teacher, Maxwell Meador, who made us hate Latin but made us feel important parsing the dead language. We called him the cross-eyed Roman because his left eye was askew, and we never knew if he was looking at us or someone else. But there was never a better man in the classroom. And on the baseball and football field, he was there for me, either shaking his head and grinning after a bad play or praising us after a good one. He even dared to take us to Rome where we stayed in a hotel with balconies. (After he checked our room to make sure we were in bed, I hopped out of bed and jumped from my balcony to the balcony of the next room. Thinking Mr. Meador had gone down the hall in the other direction, I jumped through the curtains to scare my friends, but the Roman was there. He almost had a heart attack.)

Our English teacher, Mr. James W. Hopkins, was always in a cloud of cigarette smoke and coffee steam. I fell in love with literature, poetry and the smell of coffee. Somehow when he would take a long drag on the cigarette and breathed out a line from Faulkner, words became weighty like mountains, alive like rivers. Each time he pulled on the cigarette, he would pull out our thinking. He was the first adult to ask us questions about life and the deep things of the heart. He honored our thoughts, too. When a grown-up tells a kid that his thoughts are valuable, lights go on. I began to write horrible poetry, like, "Pity the lonely intellect who soars above the multitudes," but at least I was thinking. I used to sneak a smoke on top of the library roof and think how deeply I was thinking, until one night someone followed me up the fire escape. It was the Roman and I was off the baseball team for a week.

Finally I made it through the four years and did well. I learned how to study, and because I was class president I had to give a short speech at the graduation ceremony. I was sick in my stomach because my greatest fear, besides maybe the fear of waking up in a coffin, was the fear of public speaking. I swore I would never speak in public again. But there was the sweet smell of late spring, the birds were singing and how could life be better? I had been accepted into the University of Virginia and I was going home for summer. It was all blue sky, but I was entering into the most depressing years of my life.

PART TWO

THE UNIVERSITY
OF VIRGINIA

I went to college, but still managed to get an education.

—MARK TWAIN

FOUR

Chemical Vacations

The first year at the University of Virginia was the worst. Insecurity continued to be the main fight of my life. I fell into drugs. I did LSD every weekend for three months. Going up was a blast, but coming down was acidic hell. My main drug buddy was Charley Barkley (not the basketball player). We would trip together and laugh so hard we'd almost pass out. We read Aldous Huxley's *The Doors of Perception* and were convinced a little acid would do everyone some good. When I took a trip, I felt that I was seeing deeper into the reality behind the reality. Huxley said, "The need for frequent chemical vacations from intolerable selfhood and repulsive surroundings will undoubtedly remain." I figured I needed a break from my boring life of quiet desperation. I thought I should dump some acid in the city's water supply and see what happens when an entire city is "illuminated." My parents paid for this education!

Once we were tripping and tried to hitch a ride back to school. People would pick us up and we would start laughing so hard that we begged them to stop and let us out. Trying not to laugh in the presence of strangers only made it unbearably funny. We were two hysterical idiots trying to breathe and not die. I think the humor of being human was too much for us.

The word, humor, comes from the Latin word *humus,* meaning dirt. We came from dirt. Humility is knowing where we came from and having a sense of humor about it. But humor is more serious than we think. When God was restoring the joy and the laughter to the church, it provoked more anger than tongues or prophecy, but *seriousness* is not a gift of the Spirit. Imagine, getting furious about laughing. It could be a clear sign that humility is lacking. I am not promoting drugs to laugh, but there is a similarity to the drugs ripping off the veil of human importance and the Holy Spirit causing us to laugh at ourselves and at what we thought were huge, important problems. The difference between the drug-induced laughter and the Spirit-produced laughter is death and life. LSD knocked down the importance of everything and left us depressed as death in the morning, but the Holy Spirit knocks down what is false, leaving us with an unshakeable peace. One is a cruel laughter, the other is, well, good fun.

Drugs are dangerous, not just because they can stop your heart, fry your circuits and convince you to swan dive into cement. They are dangerous because they strip away the natural protection against the spiritual world that is full of bright and dark angels. The word *witchcraft* in the Bible is *pharmakia*; where we get the word *pharmacy*. There is a connection between drugs and demonic activity because drugs give demons free access to the mind and emotions. It's like leaving the screen door open for all the mosquitoes to fly into the kitchen. No wonder people go nuts on drugs.

Demonic thoughts would fly into me day and night when I was on drugs. I hated myself and happy people. I thought about suicide. Lovely thoughts. The real problem with acid was the coming down from the trip. Acid knocks your whole system out of whack and worse, this "new perception" was not kind. I felt I was floating in a cold, rocky universe that did not like me. Once I was tripping with Charlie when suddenly he said, "I know the answer." I thought that was great, but what was the question? He said he just remembered Jesus came to him when he was a child and Jesus was the answer. I told him to take off and he returned an hour later to say he was just messing with me.

A month later, we were tripping again and he looked straight into my eyes and said, "I hate your guts. I really hate your guts," and walked away. I thought he was my best friend, and in one second the friendship was murdered. Today I believe it was an assignment from the dark trying to torpedo my destiny.

Another torpedo was streaking toward me. After the end of that friendship, I fell in love with a girl who dumped me five months later for another guy. I remember hurting so bad I tried to escape the pain by pacing from one room to the next. I could not eat or sleep for weeks. I used to think everyone needs to experience a broken heart, but now I'm not so sure. My identity confusion mixed with the rejection. I was hanging with hippies and, at the same time, with a fraternity of conservative, roll-up-your sleeves beer drinkers. I didn't know if I was a bohemian or a Virginian drunk. My only constant companion was the fraternity dog. Somehow *Yeller* chose me as her master and followed me to all my classes. She later attended all my classes at Yale and is the first dog in Yale's history to receive a diploma. More about Yeller later; I was the hurting puppy.

I quit doing acid and smoking pot just because I could not stand the emotional pain. When I would sit in a circle passing a joint, I thought everyone was judging me. Of course they were not even thinking of me—they were thinking of themselves. But I was tortured with insecurity. I went to the University's psychiatric clinic to try to tell him about my pain, but some graduate student blew me off, saying, "So what?" He reminded me of the shrink who tells his patient, "You don't have an inferiority complex. You're just inferior."

I feel like a wimp sharing all this, but I was pitiful. It was hard work being a hippie sitting around smoking pot and acting calm. On the inside, insecurity was the cold fire of hell. I felt I was not supposed to be there and everyone else was. Like my dad would say, "Well, excuse me for breathing." Once I was sitting around a campfire in Colorado with a bunch of real hippies and one guy mentioned the poor sucker reading a book on how to hitchhike. Could you believe it? I laughed, too, but

I had the same book in my backpack. I felt phony. Somehow all the hippies were in a club that would not let me know the secret handshake.

Not only was I insecure with people and girls, I was insecure about doing business, walking into a bank, or trying to tune up my Volkswagen. I had a sense that everything inside me was flawed, honeycombed with doubt and inferiority. In my Buddhism class, everyone seemed okay with the thought that God was the impersonal force of Oneness in the universe and that we needed to be free from the illusion of our personhood, but I wanted the universe to be kind, warm and personal. This was not just a hypothetical question or an intellectual exercise, but my heart's cry. I wanted to know there was tenderness in the thunder and affection in the stars. Everyone else was cool with being cool.

So how did I become free from the deep-seated insecurity? This whole book is my attempt at answering that question. Somehow I ended up in the most dangerous city on earth, and found it to be the safest place that God had for me, but I'm getting ahead of myself. It started with Jesus. I was surprised when Jesus poured His love into the deep crevices of the insecurity. I received Him because of who He was; I was not sure if He could clear up the murky insecurity, but He did. Christ opened up inside me like a parachute and where there was fear, peace flowered.

One time I had gotten drunk enough to agree to go skydiving with a friend, Clicky Gallagher. The next day, hung over, we went to the airport to jump out of a perfectly good airplane. It made no sense. It was a good thing I had a static line because when I jumped I became paralyzed with fear. I couldn't remember to pull the fake ripcord. I couldn't remember how to move. I couldn't remember if I was a person. Fear engulfed me. Suddenly, the shoot opened by itself. I looked up and saw the white canopy, like a huge flower, holding me in the blue sky. I loved that parachute. I worshipped that parachute; all its cords were mercy and kindness sustaining my life. Years later, when Clicky was dying of a brain tumor, I visited him and told him about what Jesus had done for me and likened Him to that big, beautiful parachute. We prayed together and Clicky talked to Jesus and asked Him to save him. Suddenly, the whole room filled with peace. Clicky's face was radiant. His parachute had opened. He died a month later and left instructions for his funeral to thank "Dubbie" who told him about Jesus. My sister and Mom, who were there in the service, didn't see that coming.

FIVE

Pier Fishermen

The first cut is the deepest; my first experience with Holy Spirit was a sharp laser beam to the heart. Bart, the only Christian in my writing class, cornered me against the ivy wall. I had derided him in the class for his sentimental poems about Jesus. Even though they were really bad, I felt like a jerk for harassing him. Bart was pushy, rude and the worst writer in the class, but he was passionate about Christ. He boxed me into the corner as my classmates quickly passed by. He told me I could find peace; Jesus would come into my heart if I only would kneel down with him and pray. For one nanosecond I felt a ray of light pierce my heart and whisper, *All this about Jesus is true.* How did I sense that and hear that? I am not sure, but maybe like the way sunlight reflects off a car and hits your eyes or the way a phrase of a conversation from people passing in a boat carries over water, I saw and heard for an instant, "Jesus is true." It came and it was gone just as quickly, and I told Bart to get out of my face. Walking to the car, I knew I had come close to saying yes. What would have happened? I pushed back the conviction with my reasoning. I had too many intellectual, historical and theological problems with Jesus. The Holy Spirit first deals with us through conviction, which is basically *Jesus is true and I'm not.* I knew I was not true to my own convictions, much less to God's.

I believe the Holy Spirit was present in our conception, in our childhood and in our rebellion. I'm surprised He didn't kill me one of the many times I mocked Him. I once drew a picture of a mean, old man with a long chin and nose on a white sheet, wrote "GOD" under it, and hung it up in the chapel at Virginia Episcopal School. If the school knew that, they might take away my distinguished alumni award. Once on a beach in Galveston, Texas, after a long night drinking, I was walking by the sea with a stick in my hand. Pretending I was Moses, I threw the stick up in the air and cursed at God. My drinking buddies said, "Hey, Dub, I don't think you should be saying stuff like that, man." I knew I had overstepped a line. The Holy Spirit was there and didn't kill me.

I believe the Holy Spirit was there, too, when I was meditating on a photo of a guru all alone one night on a horse farm. A friend in my Buddhism class gave me the photo and said one day I would find my own personal guru from the east. He was right—the Nazarene. I was sitting in the lotus position concentrating on the photo for hours into the night, and then the picture suddenly morphed. The face turned monstrous with demonic gestures. I'm not making this up. I rubbed my eyes, dropped it, came back to it and it was still morphing. I knew my eyes were tired but this was weird. I did not believe in a conscious, evil one, but suddenly I was aware of an evil presence and I didn't want anything to do with it. I burned the photo. I was done seeking my guru, but secretly, like Nicodemus, I started to seek Jesus in the dark, without telling anyone. This eastern god of the oneness in the universe seemed cold and malicious.

It's amazing to me how patient and relentless God was in pursuing me throughout these years. I gave Him every good reason to turn back, and yet the tugs in my heart kept coming. It gives me great comfort to know this is how He is with all of us. Lost sons and daughters, mothers or fathers, friends and siblings. No matter what they've opened the door to, God will not cease chasing them with His endless love.

God said that if we seek Him, we will find Him (Jeremiah 29:13). The desire to seek Him comes from the Spirit. There is a seeking because there is a faith that knows there is something, or rather, someone, to seek. You don't look for someone who is not there. You only knock on the door when you think someone is on the other side. So, I was knocking on the door, but had issue with the exclusivity of Jesus. There must be a way to rub Jesus into all the other religions. (I did like the joke about the Dalai Lama telling the pizza guy, "Make me one with everything.") I read books on the unity of Christianity and eastern religions but they seemed like the snake saying to the rabbit, "Let's team up," only to swallow the rabbit. Most of my friends thought all religions are equal and the exclusivity of Jesus was arrogant. They reduced Jesus to an enlightened guru, but His followers made Him the only way. I would wonder if my friends were just as exclusive; they thought their religion of all-religions-are-the-same was superior to the poor, stupid Christians who did not understand the deep enlightenment of their Master, who perhaps was not totally enlightened either.

The warmth of the personal God of the Christians seemed to better the universalism of the east, but how would I deal with the arrogance of Jesus, with His declaration that He was the only way to the Father? Who did He think He was? If only Jesus could be humbler! But now that the Holy Spirit had made the first cut, I had to find out more about Jesus, or totally refuse Him. I had to close the wound one way or another.

This led me to major in Religious Studies and take a course on Buddhism taught by a professor who had lived with Buddhist monks for three years. We had to read and bring his book on the eight-fold path of Buddhism. One afternoon I sat down at my chair, and as was my custom, threw my books in the floor. The professor entered the room and saw his sacred book on the floor. He stopped, looked up to the ceiling and said, "I will not begin class today until respect is shown to the teachings of the Enlightened one." Nobody moved and I had no idea what he meant until he said, "Someone has my book on the floor and obviously has no honor for the Dalai Lama." I picked up the book thinking, *Jesus*. I don't know if I was cussing or praying.

In another class on ethics, the guest lecturer was Dr. Joseph Fletcher, the author of *Situational Ethics,* which states there are no absolute rights and wrongs—one should only seek what is the greater good for the majority. He wrote,

> *"People [with children with Down's syndrome]... have no reason to feel guilty about putting a Down's syndrome baby away, whether it's "put away" in the sense of hidden in a sanitarium or in a more responsible lethal sense. It is sad; yes. Dreadful. But it carries no guilt. True guilt arises only from an offense against a person, and a Down's is not a person."*

I asked him after class if he thought there might be a few absolute certainties and he stormed off, "Absolutely not!" It seems people who have no absolutes also believe we are not created with any purpose; we are just chemical haphazard pools of life. I asked him what he thought made a person a person, and he said something like, "If the person serves a purpose of the greater good of other people, he is a person." So, babies, old people, people with disabilities and pastors are expendable! People need to think through to the logical consequences of their belief system. I could not quite put my finger on why his answers unsettled me, but I knew I needed a belief in a personal God who made and gave value to people being people.

You have to understand that my quest for absolute truth was not to satisfy an intellectual curiosity. I was drowning for lack of meaning. So I sat down with a professor of philosophy and asked him how he dealt with living without absolute truth. He said, "There is the rub. I do what Kant did. Basically, he just put a brick in midair and built a castle of belief." That was good enough for him but not for me.

Years later, I wrote this article about pier fishermen to explain how much I suffered trying to find God in the university classroom:

I don't want to go to the pier today. It's just that there are so many men there who don't see fishing as mysterious. When they see a hooked shark break the surface, they say, "It's just a shark." It's almost blasphemy. Perhaps they have cut out the magic in opening so many sharks, but I still see sharks as if I were seeing, for the first time, beauty and danger entwined together. Teenagers look at girls with the same reverence. It is the same reverence with God.

I remember taking a class at the University of Virginia where we discussed Mircea Eliade's book, The Sacred and the Profane. He talks about the *mysterium tremendum*, the mystery that both attracts and repels. In the atmosphere of thick books, pipe smoke, and dark wood walls, we all felt a little proud that we were reading books about unexplainable emotions and eternity. Others were selling out early, studying business and law, but we were going after life's real meaning. I remember feeling we were about to uncover something beautiful and dangerous, but the professor closed the conversation as if he were putting away the *mysterium tremendum* in a tobacco pouch. Pier fisherman.

When fishing on the shore, I have to think that I may catch a fish never seen before. I have to know that God can be known and touched in the middle of our bruised life. He made us to want that and to demand it. I know that there are a limited number of fish and the ocean has been mapped and folded into filing cabinets, but on winter evenings the waves tell me that lots of things go on forever. I will never say I have loved and have hit the bottom of love. I will never say I lived and now I am retiring. I will never say I have prayed, touched God and now am ready for something else.

So many students with sharp, hardened minds think they have "demythologized" just about everything. With an intricate system of filing, they have every passion, and unexplainable feeling, gagged and bound. Perhaps after so many disappointments, the heart just gives up and resignation takes the heights out of the skies and the depths out of the oceans. We grow up and know that the woods behind our house do not go on forever; we think everything is like that.

What is so amazing about Jesus is how He lived in such a cramped life. He never really traveled farther than fifty miles. He stayed Jewish in a mixed culture. His diet wasn't too exciting and He never seemed to dapple much in art, literature or music. He was pretty much like all of us; he lived a very limited life with limited options. But He lived trembling in the Father's love. People ran to Him and listened to His simple words the way we look at the Grand Canyon for the first time. When He touched a blind man and rivers of light crashed into his retina, people would squeal, as if to say, "I knew it. I knew there was a heck of a lot more than just getting a job, walking around the park and dying!" Jesus pointed them to something more.

Well, I am the sort of person who for years I blew out my birthday candles and secretly wished I could fly. I really wanted to fly. Now, where in the world would I get a desire like that, much less an ability to believe that it would be possible? I really thought one day I would take off, much to the amazement to friends and family. And I would fly simply because I did not waste my birthday wishes on lesser stuff. And now, years later I'm thinking I should not have given up.

For four years I pressed through the University of Virginia, living on a horse farm, going to classes with my dog, listening to beautiful but sad music and writing poetry late into the night. I graduated with a major in Religious Studies and a minor in English Literature. I had really painted myself into a corner.

PART THREE

GO WEST

I'm about to cross a time zone, and I feel younger already.
If I keep traveling west, maybe I can catch up to the love of my youth.

—JAROD KINTZ

SIX

Wyoming

After graduation from the University of Virginia, I applied to more than twenty private schools for a teaching job and everyone turned me down. They said I needed experience and I said I could get experience if they hired me and that usually ended the interview. So, I got my dog, headed west with three redhead girls, Kathy, Anne and Megan, to Riverton, Wyoming, and landed a bridge construction job. I had traveled with them the previous summer. Their fathers thought I would somehow protect them on the trip. We had camped in Yellowstone National Park; a park ranger warned us about the grizzlies that had attacked some campers recently. He told us to make lots of noise; so we chanted Native warpath songs and banged on our metal plates. When I went down to the creek to wash the dishes with Kathy, Anne and Megan hid in the bushes and covered themselves with their rain parkas. When we passed by, they jumped out and growled. Kathy, who was carrying a stack of plates, threw them straight up into the air and fell back into the bushes. If there were any bears nearby, they would have loved it.

I worked ten hard hours each day and drank three hard hours at night. We partied almost every night at the bars where I thought I was a big shot walking in with the three redhead girls. I asked a few Arapaho Indian girls to dance and came close to getting beat up by their boyfriends. One told me, "Buddy, if you are going to be dumb, you better be tough." I think my angels kept me from serious beatings. At work one day, as we ripped out the plywood from underneath the bridge, the board I was sitting on began to tip. To this day, I don't know how it tipped back. It would have been a hundred-foot drop onto a dry riverbed. I think angels never retire or get arthritis. The same angel who busted Peter out of jail must still be busy today, maybe in downtown Detroit. The next day, I stepped on a big nail and hopped over to the boss, who just looked at it, spit his tobacco at my feet and pulled the nail out with his hammer. He told me to get a shot at the end of the day. I can still remember walking around with my boot sloshing with blood. These guys were tough. The only reason there was an opening for the job was because three of them had gotten into a fistfight, leaving two in the hospital.

I was a vegetarian because I had bought into the Hindu philosophy that when we eat the flesh of a cow, we take in the stress and fear of the cow being slaughtered. Like my boys say, I was an idiot. I convinced the three redheads to become vegetarians, too. They all promised not to eat any chicken, fish or meat. But one evening I saw Anne with her boyfriend buying dinner at Kentucky Fried Chicken. When they arrived at our place we asked them if they heard about the warning on the radio about food poisoning at the Kentucky Fried Chicken. They said no, but turned pale, and we laughed till we couldn't breath.

So I was working hard, drinking hard and reading my Bible before turning the light out. Sometimes I would be so drunk I had to shut one eye to read it. With one or two eyes, Jesus would impress me. I read the Book of Matthew and would come out to tell the redheads about this Jesus. I would say, "Hey listen to this. Jesus said we have to lose our life to win it. Is that heavy or what?" They asked me if I was getting religious and I said. "No way. But this Jesus, He's something. Really, He's really something." I did not believe that the Bible was the very word of God and I certainly did not believe that it was historically accurate because I had studied the German theologians of higher criticism in college. I was educated way beyond my intelligence and I was under no obligation to believe the Bible just because it was the Bible. When a Christian would argue with me saying, "But the Bible says," they would lose me. However, Jesus doesn't seem to mind if you don't believe in the Bible. His words still cut. If someone jumps out with a knife, and you say, "Hey, that's not a real knife," the knife still cuts. Your belief in the knife does not really matter. So the Word was slicing me up.

I dated a cowgirl whose truck had back wheels so jacked up that I would almost fall into the dashboard. I even bought a cowboy hat and boots trying to fit in. Once I traded boots with another cowboy at the bar. But one night sitting on the hood of the cowgirl's car, I look up at the moon and felt empty and dirty inside, like a big ashtray. I also didn't like the cold Wyoming winter approaching. I knew I had to get out of town and pursue God. So, I told the cowgirl I was leaving and I resigned from work. The construction boss said I was a good worker and he would miss me, but the cowgirl only said, "Okay." I packed my car, whistled for my dog and drove south into the warmth.

I picked up hitchhikers along the way, and talked about seeking God with everyone. I met a Satanist who thought he had made a good deal with the devil—chicks, drugs and rock n' roll now and pay the devil later. When I asked him if could get out of the deal, he said "No man, but who cares, I will be so stoned nothing matters." Days later I arrived at Cuba, New Mexico and decided to give the town a try. Within a few hours, I had a job interview at a high school for a teaching position and a cheap apartment to rent. It was freezing, so I splurged and paid for a motel room. At three in the morning I woke up frozen with fear. I could hardly breath. I sensed something squeezing the life out of me. I had felt anxiety and panic before but never something so palpable. I just knew I had to get out of town, though I wondered why I was leaving a nice warm room already paid for, not to mention blowing off the job interview. Within a few minutes

I was out of town and the oppression lifted. I drove toward Arizona and felt almost happy.

To this day, I believe an angel scared me out of Cuba, New Mexico. Only later did I find out Cuba is a hub for witches and warlocks. In the Bible, angels are known for hurrying people out of town, and they are still active. Like I said, they have not retired or become unemployed. They are not sitting in a retirement home, talking about the good old days. They are still active today. I also believe the Holy Spirit was guiding me from Wyoming to Arizona to a little Baptist church with adobe white walls.

SEVEN

Arizona

After having driven until sundown, I stopped the car on the side of the Interstate near Cottonwood, Arizona. Getting out of the car, I looked up and saw the stars, thousands of them, and felt for the first time in my life that there was a kindness behind the stars. I sensed a benevolent personality instead of the cold purple space. I said out loud, "I am going to find God in this place." The next day I drove into Cottonwood and met a few people who got me a job interview at the Oak Creek Ranch School.

I slept in my car in Cottonwood and bathed in streams the first week, and was able to make myself presentable enough to land a job in the Oak Creek Ranch School as a teacher and coach. The school was a dumping ground for rich kids whose parents didn't want them around. The kids stayed high and no one seemed to mind. I worked hard preparing lessons to catch their interest.

I decided to study the historicity of the resurrection in my spare time. If Jesus' resurrection was historically real, then I would buy His claims to be the only begotten Son of God. If the resurrection as only mythical mush, then forget it. For professors of religion, the resurrection is mythical poetry to enlighten us to a new dimension. To me, a starving man, those professors said I only needed the concept of bread. Yea, right. I needed the real thing. The Apostle Paul said if the Resurrection isn't true, we are big suckers (1 Corinthians 15:19).

I read C.S. Lewis. I read Frank Morrison's *Who Moved the Stone*. I read other books dealing with the physical resurrection of Jesus. One afternoon in the library, the evidence finally stunned me. He has risen, indeed, and what am I to do about it? Somehow I knew I had to give up the bars and the sleeping around with girls. I had already left the drugs because they were too rough on the soul.

I was able to rent a shack for $60 a month, which included garbage pickup. The sun would pierce through the boards of the house but it was luxurious compared to the car. My neighbors were a young couple with two beautiful golden hair girls. Even though they told me that they went to a Baptist church, I still trusted them because they dressed like hippies and talked like hippies, except for a few, "Sweet Jesus, Praise the Lord." I went with them to an old white adobe building with a cross on top. About ninety people attended—plumbers, electricians, cowboys, and widows. I didn't see a single college-like person. I would go every two or three weeks because I did not want to give anyone the impression that I was super serious lest they want me to sign up. One night I went to the testimony service where an elderly lady with red hair and bright red lipstick stood up and recounted how she tried to hang her birdcage. After a long struggle, she could not hang it up until she stopped and prayed. Suddenly, she easily hung it. She said Jesus hung her birdcage. In her words,

> *"I just want to praise God for helping me this week. I was trying to hang up my birdcage and I just couldn't do it. I tried again and again and I couldn't do it. So I asked Jesus to help me, and you know, I got it hung right up. Thank you Jeeesus"*

I was thinking that God was way too busy with Russia and Asia to help a half-baked lady hang birdcages. Besides, what kind of lady wraps her Bible with black electrician's tape? Was she afraid it would shock her? However, her testimony would not recede against my reasoning. The brightness of her face followed me home. I could not shake off the claim that Jesus hangs birdcages. Within a month, her testimony conquered me. Today I believe the great, triune God said, "Let's hang that rusty old cage." On days when everything goes wrong, that testimony still pulls my eyes to the One who hangs the stars. So, God hangs birdcages, stars and hearts in midair.

When my neighbors asked me if I was a Christian, I said I wasn't sure, but I was thinking about it. Along with Buddha, Zen Buddhism, Shintoism, Hinduism, the Great Spirit of the American Indian, the over-soul of Emerson and Thoreau, and the Greek gods, Jesus was certainly in the running. For the next five months I read the Bible secretly and fended off visits by the Baptists, the Mormons and the Jehovah's Witnesses. I did go to everybody's church at least once. My other neighbors were witches who were nice to me but did not invite me to church because they didn't have one. When they fought next door, it sounded like four or five people yelling. I don't think they were alone.

I only went back to my neighbor's Baptist church because I sensed something good and solid. I was an eastern educated, lonely man, living in quiet desperation. I had nothing in common with them.

I drove up to the top of Mingus Mountain overshadowing the town of Cottonwood. I made sure there was no one near, because I went to scream. Somehow I thought if I cried out to Jesus with all my strength, I would be saved. I heard the Bible say something like that. I stood at dusk at the top ridge and cried out. I screamed again and again, "Jesus, save me," but I felt I was holding something back. I looked back to make sure no one was near and I cried out again. Nothing happened. The sky was deep purple like a big secret. I gave up. Driving down the darkening road, I realized I was more concerned that someone I did not know me would hear me than I was concerned that the God who knew me would hear me. Did my voice just spread out into distance until it fell apart like ashes of air, or did it curl into the ear of a loving God?

During this time, I hiked out into the desert and spent the night under the brilliant stars. I thought I might have a spiritual experience of some kind in the middle of the desert, but that night I was too scared to be spiritually sensitive. In the dark, the desert noises are eerie and the only thing I learned was to never do that again. But then again, there is something alluring to the desert sky at night:

> The starlings chortling half drunk, too
> From the apache plum,
> With its wind eaten flowers.
> The sun's heat stays coiled around the
> Porch columns like wisteria.
> I don't know what I am
> Yearning for but
> I walk out in the darkening desert
> To be gored again
> By the immensity of the sky.

Get it? Have you ever had the enormity of a whale, of a mountain, of a sea or of an evening sky penetrate your heart with a beauty that almost hurts? When someone asked Ahab what he would do when he saw the white whale again in Moby Dick, he said, "Praise it."

After the night out in the desert, I settled into a routine in Cottonwood, working and going to the bars and, every two weeks, going to church. For the next three months I fought with the Jew of Nazareth who just wanted to take me home to meet His Father. I resisted Him. I ran from Him. I screamed at Him and then I screamed for Him on top of Mingus Mountain. I even tried out the prayer of salvation alone in my house, like they were egging me on to say: "Jesus, forgive me for all my sins. I repent. Come into my heart. Save me. Amen," but nothing happened because I was just experimenting and not letting go of me, my biggest problem. I was saying I was jumping but not letting go of the branch. I was writing the letter but not sending it.

I remember hearing a preacher say we should shout because noise doesn't make God nervous. I agree and promote the full expression of loud praise. The Bible commands us to holler but also, it commands us to hush up. In the beginning it was very quiet and dark and then, the voice, *Ex Nihilo* (out of nothing) light sparked everywhere without switches or stars. How else could the Bible begin? God speaks out of nowhere and from then on, everything is…just is. He still speaks today but we are so noisy. The churches are noisy, especially the ones I hang around. People look for relief from their noisy thoughts and we preach noisy sermons and God forbid we leave a lull of silence in the meetings. We spend so much energy to fill the silence instead of listening to His voice speaking out of the silence. So many words and information wear us out. We are informed but not in touch and we feel tired.

Elijah had to run a long way to get to a quiet place. Worn to the bone, he heard God's voice but it was not in the wind, the earthquake or the fire. It was not in the noise. It was a quiet voice, like a man saying something very important in a whisper (1 Kings 19).

When I was twenty-three, I spent a lot of time in the mountains seeking God, but I was lost—I mean, I really got lost for about five hours one time in the Wyoming mountains. It was getting dark and I was worried I would freeze to death. When I finally found my car, I was so relieved that I could go back to worrying about being lost eternally. Paul says, "His power and deity is clearly perceived" in nature but it was not so clear to me (Romans 1:20). So did I need to go to a church to hear Him? I listened to several different churches talking about Jesus, but it seemed they were trying to make Him their patron saint of nice people. Peter found Jesus praying in the wilderness and told Him everyone was looking for Him, and Jesus basically had to tell him, "Look, Peter, that is why I am here hiding!" He tends to hide when we have our agendas, and we are left with our noisy opinions about Him instead of His voice. The best remedy is to approach Him with a stillness, without our preconceived notions of what He needs to say in any given moment. He knows the words we need.

One day I was listening to Pastor Roy from the Baptist church, who was wearing white pants and white shoes and smiling with big white teeth. I was teetering close to believing in Jesus as He spoke but I caught myself thinking, *If God wanted to speak to me, wouldn't He dip His finger in the blue ink of space and write, 'It's Me,' across the skies?* Wouldn't He at least shake the earth for something so critical? Why would He send me a loud preacher with a leisure suit to call me by name? The very next moment, Roy read from 1 Corinthians 1:21, "God has chosen the foolishness of preaching to save those who believe." It got very quiet inside me. I leaned forward. Pastor Roy knew how to leave room for God to fill the blanks.

Jesus made a big stir but He was not noisy. Isaiah spoke of Him: "He will not quarrel, nor cry out; nor will anyone hear His voice in the streets. A battered reed He will not break off" (Matthew 12:19–20 NASB). Even after His resurrection, only those who were leaning forward to listen saw Him. If I were Jesus, I would have showed up in downtown Jerusalem declaring, "I'm alive you buzzards—to your knees," but He was too big for that. Maybe He only speaks to us when we lean forward because, for some reason, our will is so sacred to Him that He would never bend it with the mighty wind of His voice. He will only bend it with the sound of His voice.

And then one night the fight was too much. I knew I had to say no or yes. No longer could I keep Christ on the border of my life as an interesting alternative. I was stressed with what my studies called the angst of existentialism. I went to my Christian neighbors' house and when they answered the door, I blurted out, "Don't talk to me like Christians, but like friends. Look, I'm in hell. I think about Jesus but I can't become a Christian because I'm not that kind of person, but I don't know what to do so please don't be Christians tonight, just friends. I need you to listen to me."

I rambled on like that for an hour and they just smiled and said Jesus had a good grip on me and laughed. It was not funny. I left in greater existential angst. I felt terrible. I went home, a little mad at them for being so insensitive. When I was about ten feet from the door of my shack, I fell to my knees and lost the fight. I could not even make it inside. I said, "Jesus, I don't know you, but I think You know me. So, forgive me for all the ugly sin and come into my heart. Here I am. I don't have anything else to offer You but me." Under the stars, the kind stars, nothing dramatic happened except a new peace stepped inside. The wind picked up around me and then disappeared. But the peace stayed.

For the next few days I told nobody. I knew I had accepted the Lord but I wondered if He really had accepted me. I thought it was settled, wonderfully settled, but I was afraid to tell anyone in case they would not accept my acceptance. I didn't know if I was now "Christian enough" to tell anyone. I went to church that sunny Sunday, and Pastor Roy was preaching on the book of Revelation. I did not have a clue how the horns, the beasts, the earthquakes and hailstorms had anything to do with my life. At the end, they sang, "Just as I am, without one plea," and Roy gave the invitation to come down the aisle to accept Jesus. I thought I wasn't going to do that because I had already done it, but I doubted if I had done it right, and while I was wrestling with these thoughts, my legs, impatient with me, carried me to the altar. My neighbors were crying. The pastor was shocked because he had given up on me. The month before, he was in my house pleading with me to pray to accept Jesus and I resisted. And now I was standing in front of ninety people I hardly knew. Waiting for the music to stop, I was staring at the white wall in the back of the church where I projected images of my family, my parents, my friends, my old girlfriends and everyone else who had pieces of my heart, and I thought, *All right, everyone to one side. Jesus is now in the center of my life.*

The music stopped and Pastor Roy asked me if I wanted to say anything. I said, "When I first came to this church, I thought I would never be fool enough to stand up here, and well, here I am, a fool for Christ." Then I felt I shouldn't say something like that. I didn't know Paul used the same words to the Corinthians (1 Corinthians 4:10). Then I said, "Jesus Christ is now the center of my life." Suddenly, I felt a warm oil pour into my whole body. I was crying like a little boy. I had not cried for years, since Debbie Cowen dumped me, and never in public. And there I was crying in front of cowboys. I had experienced love from the people in my past but this love was pure and real; it poured over me. I wept for a long time. It was a match with Romans 5:5, "God's love has been poured into our hearts through the Holy Spirit that has been given to us." I didn't see this coming. This was the beginning of becoming a Christian, the very thing I did not want to become. *Ex Nihilo*, Christ.

EIGHT

Jesus of Nazareth

I was still struggling with questions. How could this Nazarene Jew, who never traveled more than fifty miles away from his home, dare to say He was the only way to the Father? How can people who say they know and love this Christ be so grumpy and rigid? Where is the life? And what about the historic validity of the Scriptures?

I still struggled with my new identity because it didn't mesh with my personality. I was not a cowboy or a Bible thumper. What about my sex life? My friends and family? What about having a few cold beers? I was afraid the church would suck the personality out of me. At times, Christians reminded me of a science fiction movie where the aliens suck out people's brains, and the people mutter with dull grey eyes, "Praise the Lord, brother. Praise the Lord."

Before we look into these questions, I must warn you, Jesus will change you and change you and change you. He is good and wonderful but He is dangerous. He is ruthless. He will yank out roots of your heart to plant His heart in you. He is not safe. He is like fire and there is no controlled burning. We cannot ask for a little bit of God's fire and use it for our purposes. This fire burns over our mapped-out plans, burns over the self-imposed limits, and burns through our defenses.

Jesus spoke peace to the storm and when the storm trembled into a great calm, the disciples were scared out of their wits. They were more afraid of His peace than of the ten-foot waves. Later, they got so used to His peace; they lived like flames—free, colorful and reaching wildly upward. Death lost its hold and they died in great peace. No one is free to live until he is free to die. Like the planets, like the birdcage, God will not let us drop into the dark. Thank you Jeeeesus.

I started to fall in love with the Bible. In so many movies the explorers find an ancient book, thick pages, covered in dust and locked with a golden key. They read a few lines about in the days of the fire people when there were three suns and Hootchemamma ruled over the earth, and everyone leans forward to listen to the ancient wisdom. Somehow we know that what is really important, true and life changing must be written somewhere. The Bible is not in dark tombs or underground caves but in motel rooms, your parent's bookcase and in the pews of boring churches. So, we think there is nothing too eerie about it. And when we do try to read it, all we see is a bunch of stories. As we open to the first book in the New Testament, we find a long genealogy that is like reading the footnotes to a computer manual. Keep reading. It is a book of stories because people like to talk about how God interrupted and invaded their life.

The Bible says we should guard the testimonies and a testimony is simply when somebody like you talks about an experience with God in space and time. The Hebrew word for *testimony* means to do it again; when we give our testimony, it impregnates the atmosphere so that God can invade again. When we hear testimonies about people healed, it seems to create an atmosphere where healings are much more likely. When there are testimonies of families and marriage reconciled, people hook up to the power of forgiveness and fresh love. When an old lady talks about the God of Abraham helping her to hang up a birdcage, people begin to see the hand of God in their businesses, daily chores and trials. So yes, the Bible is full of stories to read and the atmosphere around you is charged with the possibility that God just may rip open the ordinary.

Before crossing over into Christ, like I said, I studied the Resurrection. I thought that if the historical facts of Jesus' rise from the dead were flakey, I was off the hook. I did not want to dedicate my life to a myth. Most religions have a resurrection motif, but only Christianity claims a resurrection that really happened in space and time. So, if that claim were bogus, I would keep searching elsewhere for the truth. I remember putting down the book and thinking, "Great. He really is alive. Now how am I going to get out of this?"

A Sunday school teacher in Connecticut told me that it did not matter to him if Jesus really raised from the dead or not, because His ethical teachings were the core. I mentioned that the resurrection and the supernatural was the main stuff of His teachings. So, was Jesus just taking advantage of the superstitious beliefs of the idiots of that day? Was He shooting the bull? Was it just fish stories? (Did you know He mentioned Jonah right along with His own resurrection, in Matthew 12:40?) I did not want to base my living on the words of a man who twisted the truth and tricked the twits.

The Discovery Channel usually deals with the resurrection by skating around the hard historical facts, concluding with some deep bass organ music of Bach, "Of course there is only one thing certain: the resurrection is a matter of the expression of faith." The underlying implication is, "We are hedging our bets but if you want to be an idiot, go ahead and believe it." I love the words of Oxford scholar C.S. Lewis, who states in *Mere Christianity*,

> *A man who was merely a man and said the sort of things Jesus said would not be a great moral teacher. He would either be a lunatic— on the level with a man who says he is a poached egg—or he would be the devil of hell. You must take your choice. Either this was, and is, the Son of God, or else a madman or something worse. You can shut Him up for a fool or you can fall at His feet and call Him Lord and God. But let us not come with any patronizing nonsense about His being a great human teacher. He has not left that open to us.*

In 1 Corinthians, Paul nails the whole Christian message to the death and resurrection of Jesus. He dares to say that if Jesus did not really rise from the dead, we are screwed (1 Corinthians 15:14–19). But he bases his faith on the historical certainty of Jesus' resurrection. First of all, the death and resurrection of Jesus are prophesied many times in the Old Testament. Now this might not impress you, but it impressed the Jews. Jesus fulfilled hundreds of prophecies of the Old Testament. It would be very hard for Jesus to fabricate Judas selling him out for thirty pieces of silver, the guards gambling for his cloak, the two crooks nailed to either side, being buried in a rich man's tomb—all prophesied hundreds of years before Jesus. The Persians invented the cruel torture of crucifixion only around 300 BC and the Romans perfected it in the fist century BC, but the crucifixion of Jesus was prophesied in detail hundreds of years before (Psalm 22, Isaiah 55 and Zechariah 12). That is impressive.

Paul wrote Corinthians around 55 AD, soon after Jesus' resurrection. Many who saw Jesus alive were still around to tell about it. Paul challenges his readers to ask Peter, the twelve disciples, James, the half brother of Jesus, and those five hundred men who all saw Jesus appear to them (1 Corinthians 15:6); "Most of them are still alive. Ask them. Ask me." This is not some misty expression of faith that floats away from hard facts.

Of course you may wonder if it was all mass hysteria. This "mass hysteria" sure caused a headache for the Roman authorities. The Romans had sealed the tomb—it was penetrable under the penalty of death. Sixteen crack Roman soldiers guarded the tomb so the disciples would not steal the body. If the Romans wanted to put an end to the mass hysteria, they simply had to show the dead body of Jesus, end of story. They could not because the body had vanished.

Now maybe the tomb was empty because the disciples stole the body. Ergo, the disciples, who were scared spitless, snuck by the sleeping guards, rolled away the huge rock without a sound, stole the corpse and started to push the new religion of Jesus. You remember they all died for their faith, except Judas, who hung himself, and John, who was boiled in oil and exiled. This means that they were willing to die for a fabricated lie. This means that the Roman guards, in spite of the threat of their own execution, somehow fell asleep. That is a stretch.

Others suggest that the crazy women went to the wrong tomb and got excited when they saw it empty. If the women went to the wrong tomb, the Romans only had to do one thing to quench the church's fervor—show them the real tomb and the real body, but they could not because there was no body to show.

Some conjecture that Jesus did not really die on the Cross but swooned into a coma, and when His body lay on the cool slab in the tomb, He came to. Maybe Jesus was a zombie. So we are summoned to imagine that Jesus, drained of blood, his flesh filleted off, gaping rips in his wrist and feet, somehow survived the Cross and crawled out of the tomb, stumbled over to the disciples' house and proclaimed, "I am the resurrection and life" and in doing so, inspired the small group to transform the world. That would insult our intelligence as well as the expertise of the Roman soldier who stuck a spear in His side and pronounced Him dead.

The resurrection accounts in the Bible do not present Jesus as a cloud floating, a glowing glob or a spooky ghost. He is a man who cooks breakfast, ribs Peter for bailing on him, welcomes Thomas to touch Him and gives them all a hard time for not believing the women's testimony. Some wonder why the Bible pointed to women as the first eyewitnesses of the resurrection, when in those days, the testimony of a woman did not hold up in court. The reason is that they were the first to see Him, but not the last.

The point is that there is strong evidence that Jesus did rise from the dead and if this is more than probable, then the other supernatural accounts are probable, too. What matters is where you start your investigation: from the closed universe format or from the open universe where the Author can step on the stage at any minute, like right now. You choose.

Back to Arizona. In the first weeks of my new life in Christ, everything seemed to be more beautiful. The church had moved from the adobe building to a new building on a hilltop. Since we were still in construction, the church met next door in a pale golden tent. At night I would go to the tent alone and worship. The smell of the sawdust, the tent canvas and the desert air was magic. My dog would just look at me as if to say, "I like you even better now." A nighthawk flew around the tent. Life was now so beautiful, still a little lonely, but beautiful.

One Sunday Pastor Roy told me they were going to baptize a few people in Oak Creek and asked me if I wanted to get baptized. That seemed too much of a radical denial of my past Presbyterian roots so I gave him a legitimate excuse. I had to coach a baseball game at the school that afternoon. That was true, but the real truth was I was not sure about getting dunked. On the way to the school, I was enjoying the beauty of the sky more than ever, when the Spirit interrupted me with the verse, "Believe and be baptized." (Acts 2:38) I asked the Lord why he wanted to ruin such a pleasant day. So I made a deal with Him. If He really wanted me to be baptized that afternoon, He would have to cancel the game. When I arrived at the school I noticed a lack of buses. I walked in the office and was informed that the other school canceled the game without any reason. I told the secretary I knew the reason. I drove to Oak Creek and made it in time to be baptized in the name of the Father, the Son and the Holy Spirit. When I came out of the water, the water was beautiful, the hands were beautiful and I was going back for the evening service in a tent where people shout Hallelujah and Amen and it was all beautiful.

But not all was beautiful in this new world. Pastor Roy was preaching on demons and new age religions coming into the region. Any mention of demons had the tone of backwood hicks hollering about the devil. I thought the concept of demons was an antiquated explanation for modern day psychosis. And to equate demons to the new age religion seemed to me a bit harsh. When I walked into my little house that night, the one light bulb hanging from the ceiling began to dim. I felt an evil presence sucking the air out of the room and trying to suffocate me. The heaviness increased and I knew I only had to call upon the name of the Jesus, but I was curious to see how intense it would grow. Finally, I called out to Jesus and the oppression instantly broke and the room brightened. I sat down in the lone chair in the room and thought, *There really is a spiritual warfare.* Sometimes I forget about the greater reality of angels and demons. C.S. Lewis said the two mistakes we make with demons is to ignore them totally and/or to be fascinated with them and give them too much credit. If I had not learned that lesson early, I would have been a sitting duck in Colombia.

The very next week the church recruited me to help with the construction. One late evening we were pushing and heaving the beams for the roof. We could not seem to make the two beams flush together. Finally, Roy said to call it quits and told us to meet there 6 a.m. As we were walking away, I sensed the Lord telling me that He was going to put the beams together. I almost turned around and told everyone but I wasn't too sure if God talking to you was kosher. I suppose His voice was like a thought that did not come through any thought process. It was just there, so loud in my head that I almost heard it with my ears.

The next morning, I met some of the guys for coffee and headed over to the building site where Roy was already. There, on top of the scaffolding, the two beams were perfectly united. We asked him how he got them flushed, and he said he was just standing on the scaffold when a slight breeze shook the beams, and from inside the building came a powerful WHACK, like an electrical thunderclap. He looked up and saw them together. To this day he claims he has never seen anything so supernatural. I think God let me see that at the beginning of my new life so that I would never doubt that Jesus is personally building His church and that the gates of hell shall never prevail against it (Matthew 16:18). Remember signs are just signs, pointing to something bigger. Over the years, I have come up against many unsolvable problems in the church, then the wind blows and bingo, the beams get together.

Still, you might ask how I knew God spoke to me? It was like a voice that came from all around and from within at once. When Jesus was on the Mount of Transfiguration (Matthew 17), the voice of the Father came out of the cloud and spoke to Peter, John and James. The cloud was all around them and so the voice was stereo. You might ask, how did I know it was not my own imagination and I would reply, "Great question." I think when it is my own imagination, the voice seems to try to justify itself, but God's voice carries its own intrinsic authority.

Well, how do you know it was not the Devil? Simple, when the devil talks he is pushy. John 10:5 says Jesus is the good shepherd who goes out in front of the sheep and the sheep hear His voice and follow Him. In all my questioning, I only grew closer to God. I believe the key was His voice. For many, times of questioning push them away from God. Many don't even take their questions to Him directly. I searched for my answer in the Bible, His words. And He led me gently, and patiently.

The devil, on the other hand, tries to push you with fear from behind. His voice rushes you, stresses you out, give you a false sense of urgency. In Israel, a tourist saw a man with a stick behind a herd of sheep and asked the tour guide if that was the shepherd. "Oh no. If it were the shepherd, he would be out in front. That man is the butcher."

NINE

New Orleans

When the school year ended, I thought about finding a better school, a better job, though Pastor Roy wanted me to stay another year for training and then take a bus to Mexico and preach. I don't remember what I said, but I thought that was as likely as selling popsicles on the moon. I wanted to teach in the prestigious Orme School in Arizona and stay with the church, but first I had a job interview in New Orleans at the St. Martin's of the Fields Episcopal School. On the plane ride over, I sat next to a tall, thin man. I tried to start a conversation but he preferred reading. As lunch was served, I bit into a small cherry tomato and some tomato seeds squirted sidewise from my mouth onto his white shirt. He was very upset and I offered to pay for his dry cleaning, but he gave me a lecture on how to close my mouth when eating cherry tomatoes. It was a long quiet ride after that and I was thankful to get off the plane. I was offered the job in New Orleans, but I first wanted to have the interview with the Orme School before making my decision. The next week I was sent to talk with the head of the English Department at Orme. I walked in and saw the thin, grumpy man from the airplane. I thought it was funny but he didn't even crack a smile. So, I didn't get the job at Orme. I moved to New Orleans. How a little tomato can turn a destiny.

At St. Martin's, I was in over my head with coaching middle school football, and teaching the sixth grade and photography.

I taught all morning, coached all afternoon, prepared all night and I didn't have a clue how to control a bunch of kids in class. The school did not have a soccer program, so I thought I'd start one. I gave a passionate plea to the assembly of one thousand students to sign up for the new soccer team. Only one hand went up and everyone laughed. I visited the smoking area where the big kids who didn't like the football coach would hang out. I convinced some of the leaders to come out, and they convinced their buddies. On the first day of practice, we had more than thirty kids. I took the ball and zigzagged, jived, dribbled it down the field and nailed it into the net. God anointed me for those twenty seconds to play the best soccer of my life. They were impressed. So, I made a point to not play anymore to keep the impression intact.

When I first arrived in New Orleans, I looked for a Baptist church but stopped by a little storefront church called the New Orleans Full Gospel Pentecostal Holiness Church. I had never been to a church with seven names. I opened the door and the music blasted me like hot air. People were raising their hands, hollering and dancing. I shut the door and was ready to run when I sensed the Lord saying, "Have I not chosen the foolish things of the world?" With that, I went in, sat down and put my new panama hat on the bench next to me. A big-boned woman was twirling in circles to the song, Father Abraham, and when the song ended, she plopped down on my hat. Again, I sensed the Lord speaking to me, "And that's what I'm going to do to your pride, son." In two minutes I heard God two times, so I started attending the little church of thirty people. On weekends and some nights, I was now a holy roller, but during the day I was Mr. McMillan of St. Martins. I was a bit bipolar.

New Orleans is a sexy place and I was burning to get married. I remember thinking that I was a Christian who really should not be sleeping around but if a good-looking lady came on to me, did God really expect me to deny my red-blooded nature? I had a civil war going on inside until I went to an evening service where God dealt with me. I went forth for prayer and knew God was asking me for the whole keychain of my life: my sexuality, my thoughts—the works. I had tried to give Him just one key at a time but He was asking for the whole key chain. I did not let anyone know about my sexual struggle, but all thirty people laid hands on me and prayed into a frenzy. Suddenly, I sensed the gold warm oil that I had experienced in Arizona, now being poured in my whole body again. And again I was in tears. After the meeting, I drove across the city to tell a friend about the experience and the new commitment. On the way over, a good-looking girl, half drunk, was hitchhiking. I could not believe it. When I used to return home from bars, I would "pray" for such things, and now it happened. I stopped the car and she got in and suggested she was open to suggestions, but I was in a bubble. I felt surrounded by a greater warmth and I told her about the Father's love and how she didn't need to look for male affection because Jesus loved her. I freaked her out and she got out, but I drove ahead, elated that something had really changed in me. I won't say that from that day I have not been tempted, far from it, but the civil war ended. From then on, I just needed to keep the borders guarded.

But I was still bipolar. I was Mr. McMillan during the day and Hallelujah Man at night. I rented a small apartment attached to an old house on Esplanade Ave. The owners of the house were a cultured couple with whom I drank tea and talked about English poetry and Southern writers. I didn't mention Jesus, just Faulkner. I certainly did not let on that I was attending that seven-word church. One Sunday I didn't go to church and Pastor Gary Rowe loaded up his van with ten church members to visit me. I heard Gary shouting to the owners, "Does Brother Andrew live here? Praise God." I wanted to hide but all eleven of them crowded into my little apartment that was so small, I would have had to step out to change my opinion. With guitars and tambourines, they started to praise God, hoot and sing. I tried to get them to keep it down, but at once, I saw the ugliness of my pride and the beauty of Jesus. I was free to sing. Gary took down the big blue container of salt I had on top of the refrigerator and poured the whole thing on my head. "Brother Andrew," he said, "Praise God. God just told me to anoint you with salt. You are the salt of the world, Praise God." Thus, there I stood, my hair full of salt and a room packed with noisy people. As they left and filed back into the van, I assured them I would be in church next Sunday. When I turned, there was the sophisticated couple, with their arms crossed and their faces scrunched, asking me, "Who were *thooose* people?" Tears pooled in my eyes. "Those people are my brothers and my sisters, " I responded. From that moment on, there and in St. Martins of the Field Episcopal School, I was one person, Mr. McMillan, disciple of Jesus.

One Wednesday night I arrived at church with my Bible, my notebook and a hunger for the Word, but Pastor Gary said we weren't having church that night. Instead, he was sending us out in teams of two to visit the people who had come to church but did not return. I was the last person to receive a name and an address, but there was no one left to pair up with me, so I headed out alone and scared. The address was in a dangerous part of town and as I climbed up the unlighted staircase to the apartment, I thought I might die a martyr. When I knocked on the door, a huge man with a sleeveless T-shirt, tattoos and a cigar in his mouth opened the door and asked what I wanted. What I wanted was to not be there but I told him I was from the church where he visited once. I felt like a choirboy with a lace collar. After about five minutes he finally invited me in and offered me a beer. I needed it, but thought it might confuse the purpose of the visit. I don't remember much of the conversation but three and a half hours later, we were praying and crying kneeling on the floor. We were both surprised. We somehow knew Jesus was in the room with us. As Thomas Merton wrote, "The gate of heaven is everywhere." When I left around midnight, I was ecstatic. The roads were empty driving home and I knew I had to get up early the next day but I didn't care. I had so much joy that I jumped out of the car at a red light and danced around it twice. I learned the joy is in the going. Two-thirds of God's name is Go, and in the going God shows up.

Pastor Gary asked me to preach in a retirement home and it was a disaster. I was too nervous. I thought I would preach on what I was studying in the Bible, Ezekiel 37: "Will these bones live again?" I actually preached on that question to the handful of old people sitting in wheelchairs. Gary just shook his head and said I could have picked another part of the Bible. You think? As my sons say, "Dad, you were an idiot."

I cannot say I was led by God to apply to Yale Divinity School but I was accepted and told my school I was leaving at the end of the year. The other teachers thought I must be smart, especially after one particular morning. One night I happened to look up the word *laconic*, and the very next morning, about five teachers were working on a crossword puzzle and asked me, "Andrew, what is another word for concise, to the point? I said casually, "Laconic" and they said, "The Yalie strikes again." Like on the soccer field, I didn't say anything more to keep the impression intact. It was time to go back east.

PART FOUR

BACK EAST

You can't go home again

—THOMAS WOLFE

I have never lived back anywhere

—OVERHEARD ON A PLANE

TEN

God at Yale

Yale was founded to "train men to propagate the Gospel of Jesus Christ," but now the Gospel is hard to find even in Yale's Divinity School (YDS). Today the Yale Divinity School's vision statement is, "to fulfill a critical role preparing leaders for service in church and world at a time of dramatic shifts in the theological landscape." It sees itself shifting with the shifting belief systems instead of preparing shifters and shakers. The motto might as well be, "Shift happens. What can you do?"

I left New Orleans to study at Yale. I had visited YDS two years prior to coming to Christ and met with the late Dr. Francis X. Cheney who had eyes soaked in kindness. He asked me about my academic background. Then, broadsided me with the question, "Andrew, are you a Christian?" Suddenly I was crying in an interview in which I had hoped to make an impression. I told him I didn't think so, but I was searching. He smiled and said it would be all right. I walked out of his office wondering what had happened. So, my first taste of Yale was Jesus Christ.

When I enrolled, I had a rotten attitude toward the rest of the students whom I judged for using the ministry as a peg to hang their own hat on or as a religious affiliation to do their own thing: social justice, women's rights, homosexual rights or making money in a comfortable church. In my first preaching class, I preached an angry sermon from Malachi where God promised to smear crap in the faces of the false priests. After I preached, I sat in the middle of my colleagues for their critique of the sermon. They were too shocked to say anything until my friend, Mike Carlson said, "Well Dub, it is a good thing Jesus said that where two or three are gathered in My name, I will be there because you will never have more than two or three people in your church." I should have read the book of James where it says, "The anger of man will not work the righteousness of God." (James 1:20) My self-righteous anger stunk.

I am indebted to many dedicated professors, especially Dr. Rowen Greer, Dr. Timothy Luke Johnson and Father Henri Nouwen, who challenged me to think hard with compassion. Henri Nouwen, the Domitian priest, always packed his class: Compassion 101. Imagine taking a class on compassion. The first day he said, "I just read a book, *I'm okay, You're okay*, but I think our message should be, "I'm not okay and you're not okay, but that's okay!" He had me. He told me that I was okay for an evangelical and I said he was okay, too, for a Roman Catholic priest. Twice a week a small group of us would gather to listen to Henri break the bread of the word and pray in a little stone chapel underneath the classrooms. The smell of the candles, his thick Dutch accent, his eyes glistening behind his dirty glasses and the way he paused his finger over a passage he just read from the Gospels—all a strong invitation to listen to the ancient God of Abraham. He was a mixture of Stevie Wonder swaying to music behind sunglasses and an Italian chef kissing his fingers to the flavor of Rigatoni. Some people don't just teach the Word, but let us taste it, making us all the hungrier.

One day my friend, Karen, brought her Hindu friend to our small class. She started the discussion by challenging my belief in Christ as the only way. She asked me if I thought her Hindu friend was going to hell unless he changed his religion. I just wanted to come to class, take some notes and go home. I took a deep breath, prayed for a dose of wisdom and said, "Look Karen, I don't run the entrance examination in heaven, but I do know this. Jesus Christ did not live a perfect life, die a horrible death and rise again on the third day just to give me an opinion. He did it to give us all abundant life." She stared at me in silence. It was one of those rare times when you actually change somebody's mind in an argument.

In our world today, intolerance is the new sin, the only sin. There are no other sins because there is no judge. Now we are only intolerant of intolerance. This new tolerance would like to relegate churches into museums and Jesus' great commission into a plea to go into the whole world and be nice. I have been asked why Christians do a good job fighting racism but judge other religions, and my answer is to make a distinction between intolerance against people and intolerance against religions. We must honor the wonderful humanness of every single person while proclaiming the one way of Christ. Yes, I am intolerant of any religion that would muddle the call to come home to Father through the Son. Those who call me intolerant are intolerant with me. If Jesus did not rise from the dead, I would agree, my insistence on the exclusivity of Christ would be shameful.

Bishop Stephen Neill, the famous Anglican Bishop to India and Scottish scholar, lived on campus at Yale in his closing years. I would have tea with the Bishop weekly and he would challenge me to measure myself in seven areas on a 1–5 scale: 1. Bible reading; 2. prayer; 3. study; 4. order in daily life; 5. sexual purity; 6. exercise; and 7. responding well to pressure. The pressure was having to report back to him. Sometimes I would knock on his door and he'd tell me to go away. Others times he would invite me in, make tea and talk about God, Yale and nobility.

Once I was having lunch in the school dining hall with a visiting Methodist alumnus who was giving me a hard time for believing in the born-again experience. Right then, the Bishop sat down with us. The Bishop was a god of scholarship to my friend. He was overwhelmed that the great Bishop Neill had sat down with us. When Bishop asked him where he was from, he responded, "I'm from St. Paul."

"You know," Bishop Neill said, raising his voice, "I preached in a church once in St. Paul. At the end of the service, a girl about fourteen years old came forward crying. She had been born from above. Isn't that marvelous?" The man spurted, "I...ss..suppose so." The Bishop left, and I had the grace to say nothing, but my sandwich tasted better than the crow he was eating.

What in the World is Weltanschauung?

At Yale, we used words like *weltanschauung* which is German for "worldview". We pronounced it with great reverence as if we were privy to some deep insight. We thought we were a little smarter for talking about weltanschauung, metaphysical presumptions, the cognitive orientation of life and the normative postulates. Before your eyebrows get knotted together, we were just talking about how we see life through an understanding. Basically, there are two worldviews: One with God as Creator and Sustainer. The other with no God, or with a god who doesn't care and is on vacation.

The problem is that Christians don't think about it. People argue over abortions with non-Christians but there is no real dialogue. There is no give and take of ideas and few change their minds through a heated argument. I have never heard a pro-choice person say, "Yeah! You are right. I was just thinking about the rights of the woman for her own body, but I wasn't thinking about the rights of the baby's little body. I am changing my opinion."

Why doesn't that ever happen? The same is true of homosexuality, premarital sex, same-sex marriage or socialism. The issue is not a lack of heart or a bright mind; the issue is his or her worldview. Democrats think Republicans are mean and Republicans think Democrats are idiots. Dialogue is useless unless it deals with worldviews. Instead of trying to argue about the issues, we need to proclaim and demonstrate that Jesus reigns. That is worldview preaching. In the United States, the world is changing the worldview of the Christians. They see Jesus as a little private religion and not the universal King. More and more, Christians think like Oprah because they are not thinking for themselves. Also, there are many "born again" Christians in America but very few Christians who are different. We avoid our enemies, get mad in traffic, watch tons of television and act greedy like everyone else. Where is the difference? The divorce rate is lower in the church, but still epidemic. If we want to save the sanctity of marriage, maybe we should start with our own marriages. If we want prayer in the school, maybe we should get prayer back in the church. We need to teach and demonstrate the Kingdom is at hand. The kingdom is not church, but it is His dominion over all of creation, politics, history, life and sleep. Jesus is Lord of the *weltanschauung*.

I was raised and saturated in the secular worldview. As a boy I went to a Presbyterian church that had little sway on my way of seeing the world. Lots of churches use "God-words" like grace and salvation but are totally divorced from Biblical context. I grew up thinking evolution was true simply because I was told smart people believe in evolution. Since I was smart (so I thought), I was an evolutionist. I never studied it. I never thought too much about unborn babies but drifted along with the freedom-of-choice thought. When I first saw a lady, Alice Ayers, in the church weeping for the unborn, I thought she was one of those weird intercessors. Later she made a lot of sense. When I read a dialogue between the creation scientist and the evolution scientist, both sides lose me. But it all comes down to the final question: "Do you believe in a personal infinite God who is really there and involved in His creation?" D. L. Moody said that for every one hundred men who are hacking at the branches, only one hacks at the root. Christians need to start hacking at the *weltanschauung*.

Not many Christians in America are socialists and I know few that are Democrats. God is not a Republican, but many people who were Democrats—once they are born again—wake up one morning just a little more Republican because Christians believe the person is more important than the state. If you believe that life is only physical, then a person only lives for seventy to eighty years, while a government can last for hundreds of years. So the government is more important that the individual. But if you believe that we live forever, then the individual is of greater value than the state. The state then only exists to protect the inherent value and rights of the individual, while it is the responsibility of the individual to be self-reliant and help others. Nevertheless, the Republican Party is not the kingdom of God, far from it. There is a cry for social justice in the Scriptures that will make most Republicans nervous. I am only saying here there is a fundamental division of worldviews separating the two political parties as never before, and unless we hack at the root of *weltanschauung*, we will bring more heat than light. At Yale, I learned to understand we all have a *weltanschauung* and unless Christ changes that, we will not be changed or change much in this world.

Contradictions in the Bible—and in Me

On one side there are the Christians who give no thought to the contradictions in the Bible and summarize their theology in a bumper sticker, "God said it. I believe it and that settles it." On the other side are those who find a few contradictions in the Bible and say, "Ah ha! The book contradicts itself. I'm done with it." But most of us are in the middle, wondering how to deal with the contradictions in the Bible. For years at Yale I heard the arguments of Karl Barth and others saying not to worry because the Bible is not the word of God, it only contains the word of God. That was not helpful. I felt like I was arguing with my wife who says, "Ignore what I say and just understand what I mean."

So how do we deal with the God in the Old Testament who throws stones at the bad guys and the God of the New Testament who refused to throw one at the adulterous lady? We teach our kids not to throw stones and we see God asking an angel to hand him another big one. I dare you to teach Joshua 10:11 to some first graders. How does Paul saying in Philippians 4:6 "Be not anxious about anything," mesh with "I have anxiety for the churches" (2 Corinthians 11:28, author's paraphrase)? He tells me to rejoice always in 1 Thessalonians 5:16 and then to weep with those who weep in Romans 12:15. How do we handle the contradiction between free will and predestination? The Bible teaches both. The church has had some real bar fights over that. We are like a kid opening up an old watch and wondering how the little wheels can move in opposite directions but work together to move the clock's hands forward. I've learned to embrace the contradictions. It's not for me to iron them out, it is for me to trust God that it all works together like that little watch. Even the Bible is part mystery, drawing us into faith.

My real problem with the Bible is not where it is confusing but where it is clear and especially where it clearly contradicts me. Like a ship arguing that the lighthouse is off course, each century has its critics disdaining Scriptures for being off the contemporary course. When people say, "Hey, we are in the 21st century you know," I ask them what does time have to do with it? It is like saying the ocean is blue and someone responds, "No way. It's four o'clock, you know." Voltaire hated Christ, saying, "Curse the wretch!" He was sure his enlightening books would destroy the Bible, boasting that within twenty years Christianity would be no more. He probably said, "Hey, we are in the 18th century, you know." Soon after his death, the house where he published his writings became the depot of the Geneva Bible Society. I don't remember seeing a copy of his *Dictionnaire Philosophique* on anyone's coffee table lately.

I did not have much free time to feel lonely but when I did, loneliness hit me like a brick. I was twenty-seven with no wife in sight. On the YDS campus, most women were the militant, women's rights kind of women. Like my dad said when he dropped me off at the school, "Looks like you could have a good women's rugby team." One night I remember sitting out on the porch looking up at the stars and complaining to God about how sick I was of being single. The words from Psalm 73:25 streamed into my mind, "Whom do I have in heaven but Thee? And besides Thee, I desire nothing on earth." (Author's paraphrase) On that cold winter night, the starlight warmed my heart. I learned it is okay to complain to the Lord if we do it with an open hand, not a closed fist.

The day before graduation, the administration office called me to ask if my dog was attending the graduation ceremony. I said for sure, since she had audited every class. To this day people remember Yeller, but not me. During the ceremony, the Dean read the diploma made especially for my dog, *Canem Laude Fidelum*. Yeller received a standing ovation, with the local news broadcasting the event. She is the only dog to have received a diploma from Yale to this day. I got one, too.

ELEVEN

New Jersey

Deacons, Demons and The Death of a Dog

While most of the third year students at Yale Divinity had their plans marked out, I had no idea where to start looking. One night, while blaming myself for not planning the future more, I was reading Jeremiah, who often helped me in hard times because his life was such a mess. Jeremiah 29:11 jumped off the page: "I know the plans I have for you. Plans for good and not for evil and to give you a future and a hope." (Author's paraphrase.) The anxiety turned into excitement and the very next day I met the Rev. Moon, that is, Calvin Moon of the American Baptist Churches. He put me in touch with the church in Allentown, New Jersey, which was looking for a pastor. I drove down to Allentown to scout out the town before the interview with the pulpit committee. The very moment I drove into town, I knew God was planting me there, but as I walked down Main Street with beautiful homes on each side, I wondered why I was called there. As I said before, these homes seemed asleep in perfect bliss. I wanted to go where I was needed. Later I got to know each one of the families in the homes and each one of their secret pains. As Tolstoy wrote, "Happy families are all alike; every unhappy family is unhappy in its own way." Every house had a unique pain.

The church had fired several of the previous pastors. They let me know the last pastor they fired had a dog, a Japanese car and West Virginia roots. They noticed my Nissan parked outside, my dog on the porch and my hillbilly accent. They said I was starting with three strikes against me. But we hit it off and within a few hours I knew that they knew that I knew that they knew I was their next pastor.

Within the first two months, the head deacon and two other church members died. The head deacon's wife, Laura Stewart, had a seasoned faith that permeated everything she did. She would answer the phone with a cheerful, "Praise the Lord, Laura speaking," and it never seemed phony. On the morning following the death of her husband, I went early to her house. She opened the door with her eyes red from crying all night and greeted me, "His mercies are new every morning." I felt I was in the shallow end of the pool of faith and she was in the deep end.

These people were teaching me how to go out into the deep where my feet didn't touch the bottom. Then the death of an elderly man. His widow pointed her finger in my face saying, "All these people are dying because you are here!" God was teaching me to love hurting people.

Mark was the first convert, coming down the aisle on Sunday morning, aching to be free from drinking. He got so excited about Jesus, he went to the bar Sunday night to tell all his friends and got roaring drunk. Early the next morning, Mark, hung over and remorseful for getting drunk, pounded on my door. He said he had tried to get free from drinking with AA and with counseling. He had hoped Jesus would set him free, but now it didn't seem so. I did not know what to say, so I prayed for him something like, "Lord Jesus, set my brother free." Mark jumped up and yelled, "I'm free," and drove away. I went back to bed thinking, *Yea, right.* But Mark stayed sober and on fire for Jesus. The next week his brother fell from a bridge; it was never clear if he jumped or slipped or was pushed. When I told Mark the news he fell in pieces and all the pieces fell into Jesus. I watched Mark, a new believer, embrace Jesus under the stars.

Mark stayed steady and became my right hand man. He had a way of putting his arm around everyone in town and telling them how much he and Jesus loved them.

When I started pastoring the church in Allentown, I still struggled with preparing sermons. I still get nervous before preaching but as they say, "Puppies are not afraid of lions but big dogs are." I think it is okay to feel the weight of the high responsibility of preaching, but we need to face our lions. I like the story of the boy who, for three nights straight, woke up in a cold sweat from nightmares of a lion chasing him. He shared this with his pastor, who told him the next time he had the dream to turn around, confront the lion and ask him his name. The boy was not sure if he would remember that in the dream, but the next night when he had the same dream of the lion, he remembered his pastor's words. So, in the dream, the boy stopped running, turned around and asked the lion his name. The lion stopped, stood up and said, "I am your courage. Why are you running from me?" I have found talking to lions works. So I preach to myself before preaching to others.

The church had about thirty people when I started, but people came to see the young pastor fresh out of school. During the first deacon's meeting, they let me know they were the bosses. Pastors come and go, but deacons are forever. Amen. But they were happy with me and the church grew to about 120. I thought I was a great pastor, until the demons showed up.

Demons in the Police Station

I would cringe when Pastor Roy in Arizona talked about demons because I thought Jesus was dealing with psychological aberrations. You know Jesus was a little country, so I gave Him some slack about tossing out demons. Over time I bought into the Biblical worldview of angels and demons but still tried avoid the subject of demons. The topic embarrassed me.

During the dog days of my second summer as pastor, I had settled into a routine and nothing new seemed to be happening. After one evening service, two young men, Chris and Mel, stayed to talk to me about living with their girlfriends. They wanted to "do it right," move out and then get married, but they had no money for another apartment. I invited them to live with me in the parsonage.

After they moved in odd things began to happen. Mel, a big carpenter, woke me up at midnight to say something grabbed him by the throat and lifted him from the bed. Then we heard weird noises coming from the Chris' room. We woke Chris up but he was unaware of anything unusual. The following nights we woke up to the sounds of Chris screaming. We would wake Chris with our hair standing up on the backs of our necks, and he wondered why we were bothering him.

Later that week, Chris flipped out. He had a fight with his girl-friend and called me at the church during our annual business meet-ing to tell me he had kidnapped his girlfriend's daughter and was going to kill her. He had a loaded gun and an empty head. As never before, I felt a mixture of authority and anger, and I commanded him to take the girl home. He hung up and did so, but he called again and said he was on the way over to kill me. I forgot about the authority I had a few minutes ago and thought as long as I kept him on the phone (before the days of cell phones), he couldn't shoot me. But he hung up. I had to tell everyone in the business meeting—where nothing exciting happens—that it was time to leave because a crazy man was coming over to shoot me. They were furious and said they never had any problems like this until I became the pastor. "Me neither," I said.

The police caught Chris, handcuffed him to a bench at the police station and called me because he would not stop screaming. I called Mel and Mark to accompany me. As soon as we saw him shriek-ing in the middle of seven policemen, Mark declared, "Pastor, he's got a demon! He's got a demon!" I tried to calm Mark down, but now Chris was really screaming. Mark and Mel jumped on Chris to hold him down while I bent down near his ear and whispered so the police would not hear me, "If you are a demon, please come out." That seemed to irritate Chris, or rather the demon, even more. Suddenly his voice changed into a deep guttural tone, "Andrew, I am not coming out. I'm going to kill him." Then the normal voice of Chris yelled, "Help me, He's choking me" and the demon responded, "I'm not coming out." This went on for a few minutes. The police were frozen with fear. Mel quietly said, "Pastor, the demon said he is not coming out; so let's go home."

I stepped back and suddenly sensed Jesus at my side as big as a house. He was like a shadow of a cloud on a summer day. I felt love for Chris and, at the same time, disdain for the cruel spirit. "You must come out," I said pointing with my thumb to Jesus at my side, "because I am commanding you in the name of Jesus." Instantly, Chris began to cough violently and spit out a large ball of saliva and blood. This was not pretty, but the atmosphere in the police station was rinsed with light. Chris was now sitting calm and peaceful. All the tension and heaviness left. The police were scared and asked, "What the heck was that?" I told them it was just a demon, as if I casted out demons every Tuesday. We prayed for Chris and I went back to the house alone, scared.

I knew the spiritual world was real and that night I was afraid that at any second a demon or an angel was going to jump out of the closet, split the air and give me a heart attack. Nothing else happened on that hot summer night. But it sure seemed like anything could happen.

The very next day my dog died.

When I arrived in Allentown, my dog was part of the deal. Yeller was the fraternity dog of Alpha Tau Omega at the University of Virginia. There were over fifty members and Yeller knew who belonged to the house and barked at the rest. She started following me to class; soon, Yeller was my dog. Part German Shepherd and part Weimaraner, I would just tell people she was an Australian Waterhound and trained her to bark like crazy when anyone even whispered "kangaroo." She had a vocabulary of more than seventy words and read my expressions.

She attended my classes at Virginia, traveled west with me, waited outside bars for me, and attended all my classes at Yale Divinity School. I still have her diploma in my office on the wall. The day I confessed Jesus in the Arizona church, I came back to the house and she seemed to look at me differently, her head tilted, as if to say, "Finally."

Though it's been over thirty years, I still feel the weight of carrying her in a large trash bag to bury her in the backyard. I pretty much grieved alone because the folks thought a pastor should not grieve deeply over a pet.

Like Adam naming the animals, despite so much pure joy of the lovely creatures, the animals could not complete the circle of relationship. Where there is a home where the dog is the center of love, it is because hearts have stopped hoping to love. Adam went on hoping for that something more and got Eve. The glory of speaking, listening and knowing began to blaze in his heart. She was almost just like him and yet, the difference was deep and wonderful. We need people and in a way, even the deepest human relationship is not enough; sometimes when we speak our deepest thoughts, nothing comes back from the other person, like a dropped stone that never reaches the bottom of a well. Then we need to be like dogs, looking at their master; "As the eyes of servants look to the hand of their master…so our eyes look to the Lord our God" (Psalm 123:2 NASB).

Maybe I loved that dog too much. But love is like a place on the trail where you decide to either go back or go on. It can wound the heart to say, "That's it. No more." Or it can awaken the heart to yearn for a greater love. So in times when we hurt from the end of whatever relationship, it can deepen our heart to say, "There must be more. I am longing for more. I have hunger and there is bread. I have this longing and there must be love."

We have had other dogs. My family adopted George, a small

Colombia street dog who shook for the first five days under our bed. Finally, our family of four bathed him with enough love to calm his nerves into heroic courage. Within months, he would chase big dogs off the lawn and greet us at the door, exploding with happiness. If love can do that for a dog, I tell my church, imagine what it will do for people. A neighbor ran over George on a Sunday morning. A few hours later, I was preaching with a lump in my throat.

The next dog was Sadie, in honor of my first Sunday school teacher, Miss Sadie. She was a white, mutt Labrador who greeted us at the door with convulsions. I took a video of her greetings and showed it to our usher team, saying, "This is how we should greet people." Cancer took her leg and then took the rest of her. You wonder how many dog deaths you can take, but dogs do make us a little kinder. Our current dog is Eddie, who we rescued from the streets. Eddie likes to chase motorcycles and get in fights. He has no desire to try to please us like the other dogs, but he is funny. But because he is ornery, we have to keep him inside. If he had an obedient heart, he would have more freedom. So true for us all.

The day after Yeller died, the deacons let me know they did not like their pastor casting out demons of people in the police station. I wanted to tell them it was better to cast out demons than to keep them, but I stayed quiet. I closed the door to my little office in the basement and let the tears flow. On the radio was a song I never had heard before or since; "I love my family, I love my friends, but Jesus you are the center of my life." Hot white love erupted from the center of my heart. I never had felt so deeply in love with Jesus. I wish I could worship like that more often.

The spiritual battle seemed to intensify. We had Christian Stephens, the Christian version of Simon and Garfunkle, sing in our church a few weeks later. One of the duos, Mike Shaw, later became a dear friend. That night nine people came forward to receive Christ and I thought we were in revival, but the next day the deacons let me have it. I thought they would be excited but they felt too many weird people were invading the church (and some of these weirdos were raising their hands in worship). Then the deacons mentioned again how embarrassed they were by the incident with the demons in the police station. These were good men, but when they got together they were deacon-possessed.

God continued to move me into unchartered waters. Irene, a missionary to India, spoke at our church. She told us about how she was dying of a brain tumor and was being sent home. She said she was not going home nor going to die. She confessed Romans 8:2 over and over:

For the law of the Spirit of life in Christ Jesus hath made me free from the law of sin and death.

Then she paused. I asked her what happened. She said, well, the tumor died.

That sparked a hunger for healing. Though theologically I was against seeing healing as the frequent will of God, I wanted to see His power. I was studying the Scriptures to "prove" that healing was not in the atonement. But as I read the contorted argument of a Baptist theologian explaining Matthew 8:17 KJV ("That it might be fulfilled which was spoken by Esaias the prophet, saying, Himself took our infirmities, and bare *our* sicknesses,") not to mean what it meant, I was convinced against my will that it was His will to heal us. On this new revelation, I went to the hospital to pray for a man. He died the next day. Then I prayed for my friend, Mark, who had a high fever. God healed him and I was shocked—so shocked that I came down with a high fever that very day. But I pressed on to see healing and it came in spurts.

A young married woman, Martha, was suffering from MS. She was almost blind, paralyzed in both legs and in one arm. During a time for healing in our church, she felt a burning sensation in her leg but no change. We kept praying for her until the day she called me and said she was healed. She was just lying on her side when she felt a fire shoot through her right side and suddenly she could see. Then she stood up on her atrophic legs and began to dance. I said I didn't believe it. I drove over to her house to find her standing in the door way smiling. She invited me in to see her play the piano and cry. I had never seen a miracle like that. The next Sunday I told the church about the miracle and had Martha walk down the aisle. It took the air out of the room. As beautiful as the miracle was, the enemy muddied it. Martha a week later came to the office and told me she wanted to leave her husband and marry me. I told her she could believe God for the miracle of her marriage, especially after the miracle healing she had experienced. She never came back to church but kept her healing. This taught me to never stop at the healing of the body. Go for the heart.

Then came the question in the church about buying new choir robes. Some argued we needed to buy the robes with the crosses hanging around their necks; the other side thought the crosses seemed too Catholic. The lines were drawn. They asked me to pick a side: cross or cross-less? I said I thought we should all just carry the Cross and get over it, but they didn't. I unwisely called a meeting to talk about it; one side sat on one side of the room and the other side sat on the other side. Things got heated and climaxed with the choir director, who was normally a very loving man, picking up the big bronze cross on the altar, yelling, "If you don't want a cross on the choir robes, then let's just throw this cross out." I thought he was going to bean someone with the Cross. Imagine the local newspaper front page: *Church Members Knocked Unconscious by the Cross.* The church had a long history of conflict and I felt helpless to heal her. I had very little understanding of the spiritual conflict lurking behind personal conflict, and my lack of wisdom didn't help matters. For the next six years, one conflict followed another. I hated it when people told me they were leaving the church because they could not take the stress of the fighting. I wanted to leave, too.

Every Sunday, we had two meetings, which only accented the

division in the church. At the 11 a.m. service, we had the traditional three-hymns and harangue. The 7 p.m. service was more charismatic. After worshipping for a while, I would teach a more in-depth message and then pray for the sick and the hurting. Though we would see God heal the sick and free the oppressed, I felt like I had two different churches, which were drifting further apart every day. I would have liked to have had more wisdom and to had tied the boats together. I always hoped the charismatic renewal would renew the denomination, but never in history had a denomination been renewed. The charismatic groups are pushed to the side and tolerated, but never embraced. God renews people, sometimes churches, but seldom, if ever, denominations. I appreciated the American Baptist Church, but I knew I could not give my life trying to renew a denomination. Something was blowing in the wind.

I loved the writings of the Desert Fathers, Thomas Merton, Henri Nouwen and St. John of the Cross. They talked about solitude being the place where the thoughts of God become clear like tall trees. As a single pastor in Allentown, my weekly calendar was filling up with meetings, visits, counseling sessions and shooting the bull in the post office and coffee shop. I told the deacon board I wanted to take a four-day retreat in the mountains. They wondered what was wrong with me. The evangelical church today still has the mindset that if a pastor wants to have a sabbatical, or to spend some time alone, he must be near a breaking point or struggling with some secret sin. The Catholics have us beat here because they see retreats not as emergency measures but as natural as breathing. You go in and you go out. Simple.

So I rented a cabin in the mountains of New Jersey, arriving there late on a February afternoon after a foot-deep snowfall. I only took some food, coffee, my Bible and writing paper: no phones, no radio or tape player. After getting the fire going and eating dinner, I finally had the solitude I had bellyached for: no one to call and no meeting to attend. Four days alone in the deep quiet of a snow-muffled mountainside.

Then the pain of loneliness hit me. As soon as I lit the fire, I wondered how I could call someone. I wanted to be interrupted. I wanted to watch TV. I wanted to listen to someone talk on the radio. I wanted something to distract me from myself. I had a Bible, but the problem with reading the Bible is that it is not an escape from reality. Rather, it awakens us like a hard wind to see who we really are and what we can really become. For the first few days I was in mourning. I wanted to be noticed, needed, or at least entertained. I wanted music or any kind of noise to sooth the aching silence.

Maybe we are afraid of really being alone and quiet because we are afraid God may tell us something we don't want to hear, like "Go be a missionary." I think the greatest fear is the thought that God might not want to speak to us at all. In college once during an acid trip, one of my friends looked straight into my eyes and said, "Wonder if we are really alone in this universe." The fear of death is the fear of dissolving into nothingness. It hurts more to be ignored and forgotten than rejected and hated. That is why some people put up with being abused; at least they are not ignored. What really bothered me during my college years was the possibility of being unknown and unimportant in the midst of stark stars and cold space. It was not an intellectual curiosity, but a great sore. Most college kids worry about the future and getting a job, but I was worrying about being alone forever.

Now years later in the cabin, I thought I had this issue settled. I had become a Christian five years before, and I knew Jesus suffered my hell of being forgotten on the Cross so that I would be remembered forever. He cried my cry, "Why have you forsaken me?" That caused me to fall in love with Him more than anything else. However, I was uneasy about being alone because I still wondered if He was really there for me. When we have our scaffolds knocked away, we wonder whether our house will stand. Who are we outside of the church? Who are we all alone when we have no title as son or father or husband or pastor or boss or friend or doctor or candlestick maker? Is our faith just the psychological persuasion of our peer group? Do we really believe what we believe? Will we believe it when we are dying? How about the minute after we die?

I cannot remember any one special word from God I received during those four days alone. I had no visions or special dreams, but I do remember sitting by the fire and feeling loved. I remember feeling clean walking out into the snow. When I returned back to work, I felt less addicted to the attention and the admiration of people. And I remember thinking how I must carve out days of solitude in every year of my life. At the end of those four days, I felt God was not glaring but gazing at me.

TWELVE

The Wind-Driven Life

When it is time for new direction in life, it gets windy. When God supernaturally called me from New Jersey to live in Colombia, it was windy. God moves in new directions more often than we think, but we are often bunkered in routines where we think we are safe from the wind. One night under the stars, Jesus and Nicodemus were talking. Nicodemus did not want to be seen talking to Him, but he wanted to listen. Nicodemus felt a wind he never felt before when Jesus looked right in his eyes and said,

> *The wind blows where it wants to, and you hear the sound of it, but you can't tell where it comes from or where it is going: so is everyone who is born of the Spirit.*
>
> JOHN 3:8 *(Author's paraphrase)*

Nicodemus heard the wind in the tops of the trees and felt thousands of leaves moving in his gut. He tried to keep a calm expression, but his world was being carried away. He knew the wind was blowing and the landscape would never be the same. Three years later, Nicodemus stepped out of his bunker, claimed the body of Jesus for burial and followed Him after He rose from the dead. From then on, every day was unpredictable, wild and windy.

In my third year as pastor in New Jersey, I dreamed that I was walking toward the church on Waker Avenue. On the right side of the road, I saw six blue-feathered trees. Instantly, I knew they were tamarisk trees, although real tamarisk trees do not have blue feathers. I also knew that each tree represented a year in Allentown. When I awoke, I knew I had three more years to go. I hoped they would be easier than the first three. My life seemed to be a constant battle of church fights, loneliness and frustration for the church's lack of growth. But now I saw the coming years as blue, beautiful trees. Even the name of the road, Waker Avenue, seemed to prophetically say, "Stay awake to the purposes of God who never slumbers." I later discovered that small insects eat the toxic residue of the tamarisk trees and produce sweet honey. Jesus will help you turn the pest into the best. I had to deal with a lot of bitter people, including me, during the time in Allentown.

During my fourth year in New Jersey, a friend who pastored a non-denominational church said his apostle was coming to town and wanted to have lunch with me. I'd never met an apostle before and wasn't too sure if they still existed, but because he oversaw dozens of churches, I wanted to learn from him. As I was waiting for the apostle to arrive, I got uneasy, thinking about what he was going to say. Maybe he would read my mail and name my secret sins. Maybe he was going to nail me for being lazy or for not going to China as a missionary. When he arrived, he looked like a normal, balding guy with glasses and baggy pants. He immediately put me at ease with a big smile. Over lunch, he said he wanted to show me something in 1 John 1:1–5. He said,

Andrew, John is talking about his experience of touching and seeing Jesus on the mountain of transfiguration and after the resurrection. John is talking about an experience of hearing, feeling and touching and about a relationship so wonderful with Jesus. And look, John says he wants you to have this same kind of palpable experience and relationship with the same Jesus.

My eyes opened. I could see so clearly how the Holy Spirit wants to make Jesus so real to us. We should never let our faith just be in a doctrine, but in a person whom we can experience and behold. Right there at lunch, my life became a search for the living Jesus, a search for the tangible kind of communion that John had. It was not a deep teaching, but as this dear man, an apostle, broke the bread of the Word for me, my paradigm shifted. Apostles do that. They break open new ways of seeing life.

Over the years, I have discovered simple ways to cultivate the daily consciousness of the Holy Spirit. I try to read the Bible until my heart burns and pay attention to the burning the way Moses stopped to look at the bush. It is interesting that God did not speak to Moses until he stopped to look. It pays to pay attention to simple burnings. Sometimes I just keep reading His words over and over until my muddied heart is clear as a mountain stream. Also, I try to keep the cup of my heart upwards with expectation and notice shifts in the atmosphere, because He is always moving. The Spirit is like wind and wind is always moving, or it wouldn't be wind. Talking directly to the Holy Spirit, not just to the Father and the Son, seems to help, too, for the Holy Spirit is the person of the Trinity around us right now.

In that same year, someone gave me a pamphlet about a church growth seminar in Korea with Dr. David Yonggi Cho. I taped it to the refrigerator door and didn't think much more about it, until one day when I was looking at my "science experiments" inside the fridge. When I closed the door, Dr. Cho was looking right at me as I stood there for a few moments. God saw me looking and spoke to me so clearly, "Go for it." A few months later I was on a plane to Korea. The ten-day conference did more for my ministry than my three years at Yale Divinity. I began to dream big. My prayer life became more exciting in that I spent more time envisioning a big future according to the Word. Now prayer was like hoisting the sails to catch the wind. Dr. Cho said that visions and dreams are the language of the Holy Spirit and I wanted to be more fluent. When I returned from Korea, I squinted my eyes when I preached, thinking if I looked like Dr. Cho, I would be more anointed. That didn't work, but the dreaming did.

In my sixth and final year in the Allentown Baptist Church, I knew I would be moving on, but I had no idea where. I wanted to find a mentor, a man of God with vision who knew what God was doing. I heard writer Larry Tomzac say that to have success, one must find out what God is doing and give oneself one hundred percent to it. That resonated with me so much that I made plans to visit Larry in his church, the People of Destiny, in Washington, DC. Hearing I was coming, they invited me to a small pastor's conference with Larry and C.J. Mahaney. I thought it was God's new direction for my life, but sometimes we mistake a stepping stone for an island.

While I was awaiting the day to take my vacation and head for Washington, I heard that a missionary, Randy MacMillan from Cali, Colombia, was speaking at a nearby church, Triumphant Faith. The fact that I would go to that church was a miracle in itself. Months before, I thought the church was a cult. The pastor, Patrick Bowen, was a recent graduate from Rhema Bible School where Kenneth Hagin and Kenneth Copeland taught. I could not stomach watching them on TV, and now one of their churches was in our area. Several young people left our church to go to this "prophet" with his "faith teaching." I was convinced the teaching was Gnostic—trying to manipulate God through our positive confession. I preached against it and warned the flock. Several urged me to meet the new pastor, Patrick, but I was committed to disliking him.

Then, on a Friday night, Patrick called a prayer meeting and they spent some time praying for me. They were praying for God to bless me—of all the nerve. It was a good thing I didn't know about it or I would have spit sulfur. On that very night, I had a dream that Kenneth Copeland was preaching in the auditorium of my elementary school. I was upset they had invited this Rhema guy to our school. After the sermon, I learned he had set up his book table right next to my locker. I walked right up to him, pointing my finger in his face. I was going to let him have it, but right in the dream, God doused me with love. It was as if He poured a barrel of warm oil, much like the experience when I first received Jesus, but now it was in a dream. The love broke my pride and anger. Through the tears, I said to him, "Brother Copeland, I don't agree with all these teachings," as I moved my hands over his books, "but I love you." I woke up sobbing, knowing something had happened.

That morning I called Patrick and invited him to lunch. The first five minutes in the crowded restaurant were uneasy. He was scared of me because I was an angry Baptist pastor and I was scared of him because He was a prophet. Finally, I shared with him the dream and asked his forgiveness. Patrick told me about the prayer meeting. We stood up, embraced and cried like Jacob and Esau. I wonder what the people around us thought about two men hugging and crying, but God was doing something new. We became good friends. I invited Patrick to speak in our evening service and his whole church showed up and the Holy Spirit really showed up. I just opened the service by saying, "It is so good to be here with you all and with Jesus," and the place broke loose. I never have seen the Holy Spirit hit a Baptist church so hard.

A few weeks later, Patrick invited me to preach at Triumphant Faith. I preached about faith! Thus, began the relationship with the Triumphant Faith Church. Patrick called me two weeks later to say a friend, Randy with a last name almost like mine, was preaching in his church. And that is how I came to know Randy MacMillan; I would have never known him if God did not speak to me in the dream and unite my heart with Patrick. I think we miss out on a lot of good things because we are afraid to come together and embrace differences.

I still remember Randy talking about how we are called to be eagles, not turkeys. Turkeys flap their wings, using a lot of energy but only stir up dust. Eagles, on the other hand, wait upon the Lord and then simply open their wings to catch the wind. I felt I had been a turkey for too long. I flapped out of the meeting thinking about what I had to eat at home. If God was trying to tell me I would work with Randy, I did not hear him. I did not even say hello to Randy.

A month later, the time arrived to visit Larry and C. J in Washington. I admired these men for being on the cutting edge of what God was doing in their generation. During the conference, Larry laid his hand on my heart and I felt as if my heart was being squeezed. I shook it off, thinking there was something the matter with me. After having lunch with C.J., I was convinced it was time to resign from the Baptist Church and join the interdenominational church in D.C. That night I wrote my parents telling them I had found my new direction and went to bed. At 3 a.m., I woke up with a start hearing one word echoing inside, "No." I knew God was telling me to run from these guys, but I was disappointed because a few hours earlier I was so happy to be connected to them.

I continued on to Virginia Beach to visit my sister and I decided to visit Pastor John Gimenez of the Rock Church. He was not there, so I was ushered in to talk to a new assistant pastor who had just moved into his office. His bookshelves were still empty, except for one book. I was still confused by the "No" of God, and I did not plan to mention anything to him about the Destiny Church. I only was going to ask what God was doing in Virginia, but I said something about Destiny. The pastor raised up his hand and said, "Say no more." He walked over to his bookshelf and gave me the lone book on the shelf. It was a book written by a couple who left the Destiny People because of the overemphasis on shepherding. The leaders were controlling the people's lives. The members of the church had to have permission from their pastors before dating anyone, before taking a job or before any major decisions. I think the leaders were trying to obey God to the max, and I still highly regard both men, but there is a danger when we try to take on the role of the Holy Spirit.

When I read the introduction of the book that the pastor gave me, I took it as a confirmation. I walked out of Rock Church on a crisp, beautiful day, weeping. I was so happy to know God was leading, although I had no idea where. I didn't even know how soon I would discover my new direction. As I was getting in my car, I saw another church across the street. On a whim, I walked into the Kempsville Presbyterian Church and asked to talk to a pastor. Again, the senior pastor was not there but they took me to talk to Kevin Coyle, the pastor of missions. As soon as I walked into Kevin's office, he looked at me and said, "I don't why you are here, but I am supposed to give you this card." I read the name on the card—Randy MacMillan—and said that was amazing because just two months earlier I had heard Randy speak in New Jersey. Kevin merely said, "You need to call him." I said, "Maybe."

That afternoon I called Randy and he answered the phone in Cali, Colombia. "Andrew McMillan. I have been waiting for your call." I asked him how he even knew my name. He said when I walked out of the New Jersey church two months before, Patrick pointed me out to him saying he needed to know me. From that moment God put me in Randy and Marcy's hearts and they had been praying for me ever since. "I think God is calling you to Colombia," Randy insisted, but I told him I doubted it. Randy said, "Andrew, I remember you had on an old fedora hat, like a gangster wears, and I knew God had his hand on you." That spooked me and I hung up, thinking this guy was weird.

Randy was not the sort of leader who would try to pressure people into decisions. He valued the role of the Holy Spirit as a guide to each believer and would ask lots of questions to help people hear the voice of God for themselves. But on that day, Randy was pushy. He told me later he could not believe how he was talking to me. A few weeks later I was back in New Jersey praying on a Thursday afternoon on my back porch. I told God I would be willing to go to Colombia, but I needed a clear sign, "a Macedonian call." Those were my exact words. I was referring to the clear call Paul received to reroute his journey to go to Macedonia in Acts 16. The following Saturday, I received a letter in the mail from Colombia. Randy wrote,

> Dear Andrew,
> Consider this letter your Macedonian call. Come and help in ministry. The fish are jumping in the boat...

I felt like I had just tripped the alarms in heaven and the spotlight was on me. I dropped to my knees and said I would go to Colombia—but only for two years. I had the idea I would return to the States after two years and plant a mission-oriented church. God, of course, tricked me and put a love for the Colombians in me that has had me here for thirty years and counting. I called Randy back and told him I would like to visit them to confirm the calling. A few weeks later I was in their beautiful home. Randy and Marcy did not fit the missionary image—they were on fire with joy, breaking molds, enjoying pastoring the fastest growing church in Cali, which met in the city council's auditorium.

Randy let me preach twice; both times, I was shocked to see how many people came to the Lord at the altar call. The fish were indeed jumping in the boat. Randy then presented me to the congregation as a single pastor who was coming to help with the work. We both thought I would probably marry a nice Colombian girl. I flew back to New Jersey to give the church my resignation with two months' notice. I kept in touch with Randy to help me through the transition and he told me I needed to go to language school in Costa Rica first. I asked him if the Cali church would pay me a salary and he said, "Oh brother, welcome to the life of faith. You have to raise your own support, but God will provide better than the deacons." Randy was right again.

I visited all my pastor friends in the area and the first five pastors told me they did not have the budget to support me. I went back to my little office and started to pray and opened the Bible to Deuteronomy

8:18, "But you shall remember the Lord your God, for it is He who is giving you power to make wealth." (NASB) I had never seen that and it felt as good as a check in my hand. About an hour later, an old lady, who only came to church every now and then knocked on my door. She had heard I was going to the mission field and needed to bring me a check. After she left, I opened the envelope with fear and trembling. It was for $5, the firstfruits of thirty years of provision.

THIRTEEN

The Romantic Wind

I was busy making preparations for my visa and the language school in Costa Rica. I spent my days giving away my furniture and saying goodbye to my first church. One young man came over to my house to say he had heard I was leaving and ask if he could have my stereo, all in one breath. I laughed and gave it to him. During that time, I called Kathy Brown, a beautiful girl who attended the Fountain of Life Church in Burlington, New Jersey, to tell her I was leaving for Colombia. For the past six years, I'd had my eye on her but she kept her distance from me. She was in love with another guy: a tall, dark Hispanic man. I had met her during my first year in New Jersey when we had gone out together for dinner with a group of friends. I went home that night wondering whether I had met my wife. Kathy went home and in her prayer time God told her I was going to be her husband. She cried, "No, no, no God; not him." I just did not "turn her on." She told God she would marry me only if He put a real love in her heart for me. With that, she thought she was off the hook.

Kathy came to Christ when she was nine. One night when she was twelve, God called her to be a missionary to Spanish speaking countries. When I called her, she was in Ecuador on a mission trip. I called her the next week to ask her out for one last dinner, the last supper. With all my plans to leave for Costa Rica and then later onto Colombia, I was in no way going to start a relationship, but I wanted to tell her my dreams. I wondered what might have happened between us if I were not leaving for South America. I called her the next day and asked her out again. I was falling in love. She knew what God had told her about me but was not feeling the same. We continued going out together while I was dealing with the final goodbyes to the church.

The church told me I needed to write my formal resignation and read it during the annual business meeting. I rushed to my office and wrote out a two-paragraph resignation mentioning how much I loved them and about my calling to South America. I thought it was just a formality but when I stood up to read it, I broke. It took almost half an hour to get through it. I had known my love for the people was deep, but I had no idea how deep. The first cut is the deepest.

With still a few weeks left in New Jersey, I went to hear Lester Sumrall speak at Pastor David Demola's church in Edison, New Jersey. Dr. Sumrall asked me who I was and where I was going, and then he prayed that I would crush the columns of religion to dust in Colombia. When I fell backwards, he yelled, "Pick that boy up. I'm not finished with him." He continued to prophecy about changing the landscape of the land. I got up a little drunk and inflamed with desire to rush to Colombia. I drove back breathing fire. The next day I had been praying for two hours in the church when I saw it was time to call Kathy to confirm our date. But I decided since she was not showing much interest in me, I would just tell her we needed to call it quits so I could focus on Colombia. As I was going down the stairs to my office, God spoke clearly to me, "I'm not finished with you yet." As I prayed, I sensed God asking me if I wanted Kathy as my wife. I felt the weight of the question, swallowed and said yes. And then so clearly, I heard Him say, "She is yours." I don't like to tell this story often because when the heart is ignited with romance, it is hard to separate the soul and the spirit. We can easily be confused in this area. But it was clear as a bell. The next week I told her I loved her. Kathy responded, "That's interesting. What makes you think that?" I was furious. She was getting her Masters at Rutgers and working as a social worker; and I felt she was treating me as one of her cases. "That's interesting?" Give me a break! I remember telling the Lord those exact words, "Give me a break." He spoke back, "I am. I am breaking you."

At any rate, with the leading of the Lord, I pressed on. Returning home to West Virginia, my parents told me they were not too happy about me going to Cali. As a parent now, I can only imagine what they went through. I invited Kathy to come and meet my parents, certain that would change the tide of her heart. After a week in the mountains, I asked her again if she loved me, and she said no. She got on the plane for New Jersey and I went back to my parent's house asking God about the "She is yours" thing. I had to pack and get ready for Costa Rica, brokenhearted.

I called Kathy three days later to see how she was doing. She said, "Miserable. I miss you," and I said, "That's great!" She finally was feeling something for me. I decided to postpone my departure so Kathy could return to West Virginia for another week. During that time, I took her to the Berry Hills Country Club for dinner. I had planned to take her after dinner to the balcony overlooking the blue-colored mountains at dusk and propose to her. Little did I know, that during dinner her heart, spirit and soul had all lined up and she fell madly in love with me. If I would have asked her to marry me before dinner, it would not have been the same. So, she said yes and we kissed and prayed. We felt as if we were on a huge ocean liner leaving the dock. We knew we were embarking on a destiny bigger than we were.

We walked down the hill to the car where some friends, John and Katy, were waiting to drive us home. We were laughing and drunk in the Spirit. And for what we were going to go through, we needed the new wine. I have a simple thought for all single people:

One week of marriage makes up for a thousand lonely nights,
and one minute of heaven will make up for the rest.

I left for Costa Rica and she returned to New Jersey to get ready for the wedding and the change of her life. After three lonely months of language school, I returned for the wedding, and then we both returned to Costa Rica for more school. On the day of the wedding the church was packed. Her pastor, Paul Graban said, "Love is blind, but marriage opens your eyes." I have used that line in every wedding ceremony I have done. I am indebted to Pastor Graban for his encouragement to go after Kathy, saying, "That girl is top shelf." Kathy and I walked out of the church without a clue what God was going to do. Kathy had Ruth 1:15 inscribed inside her wedding band, "Where you shall go, I will go." She did not know what she was getting into.

We honeymooned in Bermuda, then another week on the island of San Andres off the coast of Costa Rica. Our new mission had a small church plant on the island, so I wanted to minister in the church. Kathy was not so happy that we were preaching on our honeymoon, but I thought that was what missionaries did. I thought wrong. I remember speaking the best Spanish I could, but it was a waste. No healings, no impact, and no salvations. Just thirty bored people listening to a gringo butcher their language underneath a beautiful Caribbean sky.

The next day we hired a boat to take us waterskiing so I could impress Kathy with my ability to slalom ski. I was in the water and gave Captain Peety the thumbs up. Kathy smiled as the motor fired up, the cable tightened and the power of the boat began to drag me through the water. Water surged up my nose, blasted against my torso, and pushed my eyeballs back into my head. I let go of the bar. As they circled around, Kathy was covering her mouth laughing. Captain Peety threw me the cable; I grabbed the bar and gave them the thumbs up again to proceed. The motor roared, the cable tightened and a 250-horsepower motor towed my face into the water. Water was shoved into every crevice of my body. I could feel I was not rising up. I let go of the bar again; now Kathy and the captain were both laughing. They thought I should give up, but like Churchill, I said, "Nevah." I took hold of the cable and swore not to let go of it even if they dragged me through a brick wall. No matter what, I was not letting go this time. The motor rumbled, the line stretched, and I held on for dear life. All the Caribbean Sea blasted against me. I could not see or sense that I was being lifted up; then, suddenly, I was on top of the water...skiing. I was king of the island. I hooted, waved and then fell.

Over the years I have seen that believing a word from the Lord is a lot like water skiing. The word in our heart and in our mouth is like the bar fastened to the cable. The cable is faith connected to the power source in heaven. As we begin to believe a promise for healing or for a breakthrough in some area of life, all the force of hell seems to rush against us. Things seem to get worse. But if we can hold on and keep believing, keep confessing and keep praising, suddenly the power of heaven will lift us up and over the opposition and we will be skiing on a higher level.

After impressing Kathy, I depressed her. We went to the airport to fly to Costa Rica but we did not know you had to confirm the reservations the day before. They had given our reservation to someone else, and we had to wait to fly out the next day. We also had no reservation at a hotel so we were stuck. My only option was to call Captain Peety, who was glad to let us sleep on the floor in his living room. Kathy reminds me of our honeymoon on the floor, without air conditioning, and listening to rats scurry across the room. I thought, "But hey, we are missionaries." Again, I thought wrong.

When we arrived in Costa Rica I thought there would be a little apartment ready and waiting for us. The taxi left us at the address I had been given, and we knocked on the door, but the owner who was supposed to meet us, was not there. We were standing on the sidewalk with our suitcases and it began to rain. Again, Kathy was not impressed with me. Finally, a neighbor showed up to give us the key to the little place with one pan, two glasses, two forks, two knives and two bikes. The bikes were for riding in the rain back and forth to school. And again, Kathy was not impressed.

For three months we suffered through language school. The teachers had a gift of discouraging us. One student was a retired CEO of a large company. She left class in tears saying, "I had my own company. I have always excelled in school, but now I am a complete idiot." We felt the same way. I had studied Greek, Latin and Hebrew so I thought Spanish would be a snap, but I found out I had to actually speak this language. I could read Spanish, but I could not understand someone speaking. To me, Spanish sounded like a river full of squealing animals. In the midst wondering whether I would ever be able to understand the language, I came upon a big lady yelling at her little poodle. The dog was looking at her and seemed to understand every single word she spoke. I decided if the dog could understand Spanish, then I could, too. Besides, even three-year-olds spoke Spanish a thousand miles an hour.

Then we caught Dengue Fever, a bone-crushing disease carried by mosquitoes that causes high fever, vomiting and diarrhea. We were a mess, hardly able to get out of bed. We could only laugh at all the weird noises our bodies were making. During this time, the Cleveland Browns were in the AFC playoffs with the Denver Broncos and we were able to watch the game in Spanish. Kathy came to know my addiction to the Browns, who have continued to break my heart for half a century. John Elway drove the ball down the field in two minutes to go and beat the Browns. I have forgiven everybody in my life but John Elway. Kathy has learned to forgive me and has never broken my heart. When Ruth Graham was asked if she ever contemplated divorce, she responded, "Divorce? No. Murder? Yes." Kathy likes to quote her frequently.

PART FIVE

COLOMBIA

FOURTEEN

Cali

When Randy MacMillan picked us up in an old jeep at the Cali airport, I declared reinforcements had arrived. He later told me how glad he was to have people that came with a desire to serve his vision and not use his church for a platform to do their own thing. Randy and Marcy had had a handful of missionaries come to use the church as a base to promote their own ministries. Many para-church organizations are fruitful, but sometimes they seem to suck strength from the local church for their own projects. One sign of an unhealthy para-church group is when they do not win people to Christ or raise their own leaders; they only pull leaders away from the church. Kathy and I had come simply to serve the vision God gave to Randy.

We stayed in their home while looking for an apartment. The next day, while Randy and I were standing in his swimming pool, I anxiously asked, "Randy, what do you want me to do?" Randy just continued to pass his hands over the surface of the water without saying a word. I told Randy years later that he never did answer that question, and he would respond he did not want to interrupt the Spirit. Like Genesis 1:1, when the Spirit moved over the face of the waters, Randy loved to make space for God to move and speak. He was never in a hurry and always honored silence to make room for God to speak.

Randy arrived in Cali in 1976 with his wife, Marcela. They planted the first Comunidad Cristiana de Fe (Christian Community of

Faith Church) in their living room. This was the founding of Mission South America, which now has more than sixty churches in Colombia, plus churches in Spain, Venezuela, Ecuador, Chile and the United States. Randy was instrumental in bringing unity to the churches of Colombia, cofounding the pastors' association in Cali. At first he was not so welcomed because he taught about the freedom of the Spirit, but God used Marcy and Randy to bring to Colombia the gifts of the Spirit, deliverance, intercession, healing and the beauty of worship.

I remember the first time I watched Randy counsel a couple with problems at home. Randy, as usual, was gentle and understanding. Suddenly he calmly started to pray for them. They both fell on the floor manifesting demons, but soon were set free and worshipping. I was shocked to see how quickly and powerfully Jesus freed this couple from what Randy told me were spirits of witchcraft and fear. It was beautiful to see how peace overshadowed their faces but also unnerving to see how different ministry would be from then on.

Often Randy and I would talk on the phone late into the night, until our hearts were threadbare and it was easy to talk about fears, dreams, aging, passions and dying. Like expert skiers, our conversations would zigzag down mountains over any subject: the Scriptures, the Oscars, books, politics, history, our marriages. Sometimes the conversation would turn quiet and sacred as if touching the hem of His garment. Years later, when Marcela called us to say Randy had died, I was devastated. How could an ongoing conversation just end? The man who knew me better than any other was out of reach.

The wind of the Spirit was blowing and we were learning from Randy's teaching how to trim the sails. I think I learned more from the church's Ministerial Institute of the Holy Spirit (*Instituto Ministerial del Espiritu Santo*) than from my three years at Yale. God revealed my selfish motives for the ministry. Missionaries, in particular, have a tendency to an entitlement mentality; we think we deserve special treatment just because we are missionaries. We think because we gave up belongings and comfort, we don't have to give up our rights. I once was so mad because I thought I was going to preach one Sunday, but someone else was called to preach at the last minute. On the drive home, I told Kathy how I had the fire of a message pent up inside me. She said, "Well, why don't you preach it to me?" I did, poor girl, but I saw that my desire was not to preach the Word but to preach in front of people.

During our first year, Randy and Marcy were hosting a worship symposium in Bogota and asked us to help with duplicating and selling the cassette tapes of the symposium. We were just happy to serve. Randy was preparing to speak one afternoon, but there was no podium or microphone stand for him to use. Randy needed something to hold the microphone while he held his bible and notes. Someone told me to go up and help him, so I knelt down and became a microphone stand in front of a thousand people while someone took their time to find a real microphone stand. Finally, after what seemed like an hour—in reality only five minutes—I was replaced. I went behind the platform and sulked, telling God, "I didn't give up everything in the States and come down here risking my life to become a microphone stand." Then God spoke inside my ears, "Look at the microphone stand. It is not complaining. You don't even make a good microphone stand." I told him I was sorry and ready to be what He wanted. Though I had been trained in seminary and had pastored for more than six years, it was time to shut up and learn.

I went to a prophetic conference at our church in Bogota hoping to receive a word. The prophet, Ronnie Chavez, was like a gunslinger, firing prophetic words left and right. I was in the front row. With my eyes closed and my hands raised, I thought I was giving the signal that a prophetic word would be welcomed. But I got nothing. The next day I put on a bright red tie and sat up front. When Ronnie was giving words more to one side of the auditorium, I scurried sideways, like a crab, trying to position myself. Still no word for me. Right before lunchtime, I heard the sound of rain. I asked a few people if they had heard the rain, but no one else did. I went outside to see if it was raining but no rain. I even checked the speakers on the platform thinking there was a circuit problem. Finally, I just stayed quiet, realizing I was hearing the sound of spiritual rain. It lasted for a half an hour. I went up to a special lunchroom with Ronnie and some pastors and asked them if they had heard the rain. They looked at me a little strangely and said no.

That evening Ronnie came over to our apartment-hotel to relax with a few pastors and we talked about what we saw God doing in the countries. But still Ronnie did not give me a word. On the last day, I thought for sure the man of God would give me a zinger. I was standing in the front row when a friend, Pastor Walter Rumierez, arrived at the meeting. Due to his work schedule, it was his first moment free to attend the conference. Right then, Ronnie pointed toward us and said, "I have a word for you." And I pointed my finger to my chest saying, "Me?" and he said, "No, the guy next to you." I thought that was so unfair and began to think that maybe this guy was a false prophet. The conference ended and I went back to the hotel to sulk. I did what most men of God do—I called my wife and complained, "Honey, I can't believe I came here for four days to receive zip." I hung up and started to sulk, when the phone rang. It was Ronnie. I thought surely the prophet could not leave town without giving me a word from the Lord! Ronnie asked, "Hey Andrew, did I leave my briefcase there last night?" I said no and he hung up. No word from heaven. I went back to ask God about what had happened when I heard Him ask me, "What about a word from Me?" God had opened my ears to hear spiritual rain for thirty minutes and here I was, anxious about getting a word from a prophet. Then it was clear to me—I was not searching for a word from God, but a word in front of other people. I apologized to the Lord. The sound of rain became a surety for the rain yet to come upon the church in Medellín. Hearing the rain undergirded me to stand strong in the hard, dry times to come in Medellín.

Most of the challenge of the first years at Cali involved trying to speak Spanish and adjust to the culture. When Kathy and I got married and arrived in Colombia, speaking a foreign language was like typing with gloves on. Simple conversations were clumsy and frustrating. We take for granted how we can walk into a store and say, "Gimme some gum, nasal spray and the morning paper," and the clerk understands, throws the items in a bag and tells us to have a nice day. Just going to the store in Colombia was traumatic. My West Virginia accent accentuated the problem, which was hard on me, and even more so for the Colombians.

But the struggle proved helpful, too. Once, a Communist gue-rilla fighter called my home phone to threaten me for helping an ex-commander of the FARC. He warned me to stop helping "Diego" or he would throw *polvera* on me. I knew the word *polvo* meant dust so I thought he was threatening to blow fairy dust on me. I told him I didn't understand him. I later found out he was threatening "to blow us to smithereens." I imagine the poor fellow reporting to his commander that the gringo was too dumb to be threatened. The following week we walked fast everywhere, looking over our shoul-ders. I felt sick to my stomach, but we kept on ministering to Diego. They called back to say they were going to leave us alone because Diego had left the church. However, Diego was still going to church. God had blinded their eyes.

We stayed busy with home groups and leading small tent crusades. We started one cell group outside of Cali in the industrial town of Yumbo. Every Saturday afternoon Kathy and I would bump along the potholes on the road to Yumbo for about thirty people.

In 1991, our first son, Andrew Michael was born, finally. Kathy was two weeks overdue so we went to the hospital to induce the birth. I was sitting in the waiting room for hours with the other poor suckers. I had gone through the birthing class and learnt how to breathe and walk around like a fat pelican, but I did not get the chance. The doctors would not let me in. Then they had to stop the inducement because the sterilizing machine broke. They told me to take Kathy to another hospital, where they started to induce her again but stopped due to a heavy rain breaking through the roof in the operating room. Later, they found a room to continue the procedure, and I had to wait it out again. I thought it would be like taking a number and we would be called in order of arrival, but it took a long time. Finally, doctors performed a C-section and ushered me in to meet my son. When I held the amazing little boy with a full head of flaming red hair, Andrew Michael seemed to focus right into my eyes. We were both in awe, or at least I was. I know babies are not able to focus, but Andrew did. He was not crying, just staring as if to say, "Well, here I am." I was in love.

Eighteen months later, Christian William was born and he also was in no hurry to come forth. I was at Kathy's side during the contractions to do the breathing exercises, but we would break into tongues when the pain surged. I remember I was leading a nurse to the Lord when Kathy called for me to come back into the room. I was leading her in the prayer of salvation and thought Kathy could wait a minute. Wrong again. Finally, doctors performed a C-section and they placed Christian William, completely bald and scrunched up, into my arms. I was in love again.

We would stop traffic with our two boys, one redhead and the other, blonde. Both times when we were leaving the hospital for home, it was hard to believe we could keep them. I wondered who was going to take care of them. Why does God call rookies to be parents? Sometimes the pressure of taking care of them, along with the ministerial and financial pressures, almost fried us.

One night after ministering late in a dangerous neighborhood, we were driving home around midnight. Our little Suzuki Jeep stalled. When I opened the hood and looked at the engine the size of a sewing machine, I knew the problem was the gasoline pump. There was no way to fix it. We thought we would just wave down a taxi and leave the car. When a taxi pulled up, the driver asked me what was the trouble, I told him it was the gas pump. He did not say a word, but got out, opened his trunk and pulled out the only thing in his trunk—a box containing a new gas pump for a 1975 Suzuki Jeep. I asked him how in the world he happened to have that very pump and show up at that hour. He just shrugged his shoulders and with a few tools quickly replaced the pump. I was trying to strike up a conversation with the guy, but he just said, "Asi es." (That's the way it is.) I tried to pay him but he only wanted the price for the pump that was on the box. Again, I tried to have him explain how this all happened but he only said, "Everything is all right." We drove off wondering if some angels have a little grease under their fingernails.

Another time we had just renewed our visas and pulled out a lot of money from the bank to pay rent. I had my passport and all the money crammed in my wallet making it so fat I could not close it. As I was driving into a dangerous neighborhood to make a visit, I handed my wallet to Kathy. We got out of the Jeep and made the visit. A half hour later, I realized I did not have my wallet. My life, everything was in it: my Colombian ID papers, my passport, my visa and lots of money. I frantically searched the jeep and then figured out it must have fallen on the sidewalk when Kathy got out of the car. I started to frantically ask the people passing by on the street if they had seen my wallet. We knew it was hopeless. Kathy suggested that we should pray, but I was too mad to pray. I was mad at Kathy and mad at the Colombians for not returning the wallet and mad at myself for being careless. Somehow God gave me the grace to pray. I knelt down behind the jeep. I don't remember what I said but as soon as we stood up, an elderly man approached us and handed me the wallet. He was on the third floor watching us pray and God must have touched him to return it. We gave him a reward and drove off with the certainty that God was busy taking care of us.

I remembered I told God I would only be a missionary for two years, but two years passed quickly. It was obvious that God had tricked me because I had fallen in love with the Colombian people.

I told Kathy we could stay in Cali forever. Where else would we see the fish jumping in the boat? Where else was it so windy with the Holy Spirit? The church in Cali had its problems, like any family. Some leaders were sent out and others just left, but it was a church floating on the waters. It was a wind-driven church and we were happy.

In a used bookstore in West Virginia I once found a paperback book by Paul Harvey that contained his famous radio programs. In one chapter he talked about the Swan Quarter Creek Methodist Church in North Carolina. Though the church was small and poor, it was looking for a lot to build their church. They wanted a property on higher land due to the hurricanes flooding the lower lands. A wealthy man had a nice piece of property on the higher levels, but refused to consider the offer from the pastor. So the little group bought a cheaper piece of lower land and built a wooden framed church on stilts.

Sure enough, a hurricane flooded the town of Swan Quarter Creek and the residents closed themselves inside to weather the storm. When the wind subsided, they opened their windows and saw the wooden-frame church floating down Main Street. The water had lifted the church off its stilts and was carrying it down town. Since you can't have a church running loose in town, the men tried to stop her with ropes and poles, but the church seemed to have a mind of its own. It turned right at the end of Main St., floated another hundred yards, then turned left, right and then settled right on top of the property of the wealthy man.

The next morning, the owner of the land found the pastor and said he recognized the Providence of God re-locating the church and wanted hand over the title as a gift. To this day, the Providence Methodist Church stands as a testament to the wind of God blowing where He wills. It has been rebuilt with stone, but the landmark is a birthmark that says, "What is born of the Spirit conquers the world."

FIFTEEN

The Three Letters

As a kid, I worried a lot about my dad dying. Maybe because my father was older than most fathers, maybe because of an experience I had when I was nine. I was lying in bed awake and eternity hit me like a brick. The reality of death, existence and eternity all flashed before me and ripped me wide open like a clam. What keeps us from flying into a thousand pieces? I remember it hit me so hard that I burst into tears and ran downstairs to my parents who were trying to have a nice drink by the fireplace. The only way I could express my fear was to say, "I am afraid you will die." They looked at each other, hoping the other would field the question—so much for a quiet evening. Finally, Mom said, "Don't worry about that because it won't happen for a long time." The problem was that day was coming upon us like a Mack truck…or like a bright wave.

At the University of Virginia, a writing professor took a whole class to tell us about the night of his father's death. Though he was five hundred miles away, he said he saw his dad pass by the window of his house; instantly, he knew his dad had died. He called home to verify the news and his mom asked him how he knew. We all sat in his class with chills. We never outgrow ghost stories. What really caught my attention was that his father died, and the reality that one day mine would, too.

Shortly after my conversion to Christ, I returned home to West

Virginia and was awkwardly reconciling my new faith with my old life. I spent an afternoon in the Kanawha Presbyterian church's library, that old library with books to the ceiling, where I found the yearbook in which my grandfather wrote,

> *Let not your heart be troubled: ye believe in God, believe also in Me.*
> *In my Father's house are many mansions: if it were not so, I would*
> *have told you. I go to prepare a place for you.*
>
> JOHN 14:1–2 (KJV)

My grandfather was speaking to me and I did not want his son, my dad, to be left out of the conversation, but I wondered how I could talk with Dad about it. I prayed and tried to find a way to talk to my father about our Father, but like fly fishing on a windy day, I could not get the conversation to land in the right place.

Years later when I was studying at Yale, I wrote him three letters. I laid out my love and respect for him and the whole redemption deal. I wrote how much I wanted him to end up in heaven and how his being a good man was never enough to fulfill the contract. I wrote about how Jesus lived perfectly and transfers His reward to us. I wrote about how Jesus tasted the fear of our death so we could live free from it. I wrote about my surprise of seeing Edinburg Castle suddenly lit-up with floodlights one dark night, floating like a golden boat in the dark. In the same way, Christ brought immortality to light and surprised my dark heart.

He did not write back. He never mentioned any one of the three letters.

Later when I pastored the church in New Jersey, my parents visited me and I preached, writing the sermon with Dad in mind. When I came home to preach in our family church, I would do the same. I would dream about my dad coming to Christ in tears, but he would always be waiting outside the church, holding a raincoat in his arm, only to say, "Good job."

My dad supported me when I told him I was getting married and moving to Colombia as a missionary, although it was not the career move he expected. I think he started to ask God why He would send me to such a place. When he turned eighty-one, he came to Colombia to see our first son. The next Sunday he was in church and I preached in Spanish. As Kathy translated, God explained it to his heart. He made the deal. He bowed his head and said, "Lord Jesus." After church, he told me he wanted to take the elevator instead of the subway.

That Sunday afternoon, we went to the Cali soccer game and sat high in the bleachers under the blue sky, watching the teams play on the bright green grass. We sat in a river of peace. When we got home, Dad lay down on the bed and I laid my son by his side, and they both passed out quickly. A man owns his face when he is awake, but when he is asleep, he loses ownership. His face is adrift. Now my son and my father were both sleeping adrift in peace. Peace was all over his face. He later said it was the best sleep he'd had in years.

Six months later, I rushed home to West Virginia to spend our last week together. On his last day, I sat alone with him for hours. The Cardinals and the Mets were on the television—our last ballgame together. He could only nod yes or no. I asked him if he was ready for heaven and he nodded yes. After I told him how much I loved and honored him, I prayed out loud to release him to our Father. That prayer burned deep in my throat. He fell asleep and I left to be with Mom. Almost as soon as I arrived home, my sister Jean called us to say he had died. The moment I had feared all my life had now arrived. The day my parents said was a long way off was now here.

I passed the phone to my Mom and went into the living room. I lifted my hands up. I expected the dread of a horrible storm but it turned into a soft rain. The moment I had feared for so long turned out to be strangely peaceful. I did not feel fatherless at all. As my mom was talking to the nurses, I was slowly twirling in circles, amazed by the authentic love of our Father, who art in heaven.

The next day Mom and I went to the bank to open the safety deposit box where Dad had put in safe keeping the most important documents—bond notes, titles and other legal documents. I opened the box, and on top of everything—the three letters.

PART SIX

CITY BURNING IN MY HEART

He steadfastly set His face to go to Jerusalem.

—LUKE 9:51 (KJV 2000)

SIXTEEN

The Descent into Medellín

During the year of 1991, I began to feel a love for a city I never knew. I cannot understand how God can place His immense love inside a selfish little heart like mine, but He did. I was surprised to find myself crying in prayer. When I would see intercessors weeping for the nations, I thought they were odd ducks. I was glad they were pouring out their guts to the Lord, but I was also glad I was not one of them. But now, with a city of three million in my heart, I wept like a fool.

I shared with Kathy the call I felt for Medellín and she, being like Ruth, was immediately ready to go to the most dangerous city in this hemisphere. It was also the least churched city in this hemisphere and the hub for Mary worship in South America. Even the people in Cali warned us not to go to Medellín.

I wanted to share with Randy my burden for the city, but I sensed the Lord telling me to keep it quiet for a while. So, for a year I kept the conversation about the city just between Jesus, Kathy and me. During this time, a young pastor told Randy and me that he wanted to plant a *Comunidad Cristiana de Fe* church in Medellín. On the inside I was screaming, "No way. He can't take my calling," but on the outside, I was pretending to be open to the possibility. When Randy asked me what I thought about the man and his vision, I just said, "I don't know. Sounds interesting." I was dying to tell Randy everything but I had learned we have to obey the Lord in the *what* and in the *when*. The Lord wants to know whether we can keep His secrets. We all desire to dwell in His secret place, but can we keep His secrets?

Finally, I felt the permission from God to share with Randy and Marcy our vision for Medellín. Randy told me a week later, after prayer with the mission board, that it was not yet time to go. We needed to stay at least another year in Cali. I went back to the house to tell Kathy to unpack our emotional bags. I knew deep inside it was the Lord, not just Randy, giving us a yellow light. So we waited in Cali as the Lord prepared the ground in Medellín.

In 1993, the police killed Pablo Escobar on a rooftop in Medellín and a stronghold was broken. Kathy reminds me that a week before, after a time of prayer together, I proclaimed with a strange certainty, "The strongman is bound. It is time for Medellín." A week later, Pablo was gone. In 1994, Pastor Randy and Marcy blessed us and sent us to plant the work in Medellín. I first went on a surveillance trip to find a place to start. I took a little bus from the airport down into the valley of Aruba, down into the valley of death, or so it felt. When I saw the lights of Medellín, it seemed like a thousand sharp teeth ready to rip me to shreds. Fear dominated the atmosphere. Some taxi drivers avoided certain roads known as dumping grounds for the bodies of victims. Cars would run red lights late at night because the risk of carjacking was too high. People hurried along the streets and quickly closed doors behind them.

I stayed in a run-down hotel and visited some of the pastors of the city. I also talked to some of the few missionaries there at that time. When I shared my dream of seeing thousands coming to Jesus, one missionary said, "These people are not open to God. What you are saying will not happen in a very long time." I decided not to hang with them. I have a rule of thumb: spend time with men who love God, love their families, love the people, enjoy the ministry and have a big vision.

Pastor Basilio Patiño let me preach in his vibrant church. On the offering envelope he wrote, "May the Lord make you a thousand times more than you are now," from Deuteronomy 1:11. That was the same verse a man had given us in a home group meeting in Cali, and it was the same verse Randy and Marcy wrote on a plaque to honor our service in Cali. I did the math: $2 \times 1000 = 2,000$. I made a cassette tape in 1994 about the vision of our church, declaring the church in Medellín would have 2,000 people by the year 2000.

After the service, Basilio and his assistant pastors, Jon Freddy and Antonio, took me to a typical restaurant. I ordered a big plate of every part of a cow. (A rule of thumb: never eat anything bigger than your head.) The next day food poisoning had me gushing from both ends. I had to cancel my return flight while Jon Freddy and his wife, Ruth, nursed me for three long days. Finally, when I thought I could make it home, they put me on the bus for the 45-minute trip to the airport. Half way up the mountain, my intestines began rumbling. I was squeezing my cheeks with all my might, but I resigned myself to the fact that my volcanic intestines were going to explode. By the grace of God, I made it to the airport bathroom. This was my first miracle in Medellín.

My first priority on the next trip to Medellín was to feel out where to start the church. I rented a taxi for a week and drove up and down the streets of the city. It was bigger than I thought. I began to feel a peace every time I drove by Unicentro, a shopping center well located for public transportation. When I returned to Cali to share everything with Kathy, I opened a map of Medellín on the floor so she and I could pray over it. As Kathy prayed, her finger began to shake, pointing to the exact place where Unicentro was on the map. She had no idea where Unicentro was because it was not marked on the map—confirmation that we were moving in the right direction. On the next trip to Medellín, Pastor Joaquin from the Cali church accompanied me to spy out the land.

We found a house near Unicentro that had a large living room ideal for starting the church. We signed the rental agreement after a week of hassles and headed home triumphant. The following week, the realtor called to inform me the owners of the house found out we were Christians and would not rent it to us. So, I went back alone to Medellín to undertake the search once more. Renting another taxi, I told the driver to drive by the house where we had originally wanted to rent. At that very moment we drove by, the owners were walking out of the house. I jumped out of the cab without thinking and introduced myself as the person who wanted to rent their house. Somehow, right on the spot, I convinced them to rent the house to us. That was another miracle.

We made another scouting visit to Medellín with Pastors Adolfo and Lucelida and missionaries Jerry and Barbara Manderfield with their four kids. The Manderfields arrived in Medellín first and parked in front of the Open Arms Foundation for street kids, run by Bill and Wanda Perrow. Before they could get out of the car, armed men robbed everything they had; their jeep, suitcases, cameras and wallets. When we drove up, I asked them where their jeep was. Jerry smiled and said, "Stolen," like he expected it. What a welcome sign from the devil. We decided to go to the seminary and sleep in the gym where it would be safer, but we were all uneasy. Someone suggested the robbery was Jerry's fault because maybe God was not calling him to Medellín. I suggested we didn't need to help the devil beat up Christians. It is bad theology to think problems are a sign we are out of the will of God. Sometimes problems are the enemy's flack that lets us know we are right over the target.

When Jesus told the disciples to get into the boat, they ran into a storm in the middle of the night. Some of them probably thought it was Peter's fault, but it was Jesus who sent them. Fear makes bad theologians of us all. Jerry and Barb stayed in the joy, but that comment hurt them more than the robbery. That night, I walked out alone on the hillside, looking at the thousands of lights of the city. I could feel the vision of the thousands of people swelling up inside me. Like Abraham saw the stars turn into the faces of his children, my tears turned the city lights into the faces of people worshipping Jesus.

We needed to return to the States to raise more funds and buy some sound equipment for planting the church. We stayed with our friends, Steven & Valerie Swisher, in the mountains of North Carolina. They have a clear prophetic voice to the nations and are extremely funny. More prophets would do better with a sense of humor. Steve helped me buy an entire sound system from a Western band on a rainy night deep in the mountains. The road was washed out so we had to carry the equipment, speaker by speaker, down a hill to Steve's truck. Later that week, Steve built a huge crate for everything to ship to Colombia. During this time, we dreamed, prayed like Natives on the warpath and danced in their home to sixties music. It was hard saying goodbye, but we had a destiny.

A month after returning to Cali, the crate arrived. I went to the customs office to fill out the papers. They asked me how much the equipment was worth to charge a 15% tax on everything. I paid about $4,000 for it, but I lied on the form declaring the value as only $1,500. They told me to pick up the crate the next day, but that night I couldn't sleep. Was I going to start preaching through a sound system that was brought to Colombia on a lie? Finally, I owned up to my lie and greed and confessed the next day to the customs official that I had lied. He looked at me sideways, took his cigar out of his mouth and wrote down the correct amount. It cost $600 for good, honest sound.

The Paisa is known for his/her deceptive business practice and I realized that the evil spirits of the territory would become the major temptations to deal with. For example, if a city is known for its political division, the spirit of division will attack the church. If the city is known for lust, watch out pastors. So, I needed to start the ministry in the opposite spirit of the city—brutal honesty.

When it was time to leave Cali, we packed up the moving van

with all our belongings and equipment. Early in the morning, we left for Medellín in a hard rain with a broken back window because the night before, a thief had broken in our car and stolen the baby seat. We arrived late at night with the rain still falling. I felt like an idiot for taking my wife and two precious little boys into the jaws of death. During those first days, Christian broke my heart when he asked me, "Daddy, why don't we live where everyone talks like us?" Good question. What was I doing?

The next day we were just sitting in the doorway to our new home when a neighbor warned us not to sit there with the door open. "No le den papaya" (No give him papaya) is the saying that means, "Don't give the devil an opportunity." He explained that many houses have been robbed and if the thieves see you sitting in front of an open door, you are sitting ducks. A year later, in a neighborhood meeting we found out we were the only house on our block that had not been robbed.

In the following two weeks, I saw three people killed in broad daylight. The first one I saw was with Joaquin, when we saw a motorcycle stop and fire two shots into an older man who silently fell to the ground. The gunfire seemed so muffled and the man seemed so quiet on the ground that it did not seem so terrible until a few minutes later, when the ugliness of the murder snapped us like a whip. Did we really see a man die so suddenly? The next week, Kathy and I saw two men with machine guns on a motorcycle kill a couple in a car just thirty yards away. I saw the victims, a man and a woman, slumping into each other as the motorcycle raced away. I told Kathy I could almost see the demons swirling with glee around the crime scene. I'm not sure how I perceived this but for hours I could not get the image out of my mind. Another welcome sign to Medellín from the devil.

Months later, we heard gunshots outside our house. We ran out to see three men on a motorcycle rush away. They had shot three rounds into the head of young man with a Met's baseball cap still on his head. I ran out to see if I could help the youth, but blood was gurgling from his mouth. His eyes were opened, but he was gone. The motorcycle circled back around to confirm the kill and Kathy, the New Jersey girl, yelled, "There go the killers! Get them! Get them!" She was furious. Everyone told her that was the last thing she should have done, but the righteous indignation burning in her drives out fear…and sometimes good sense.

The police came to pick up the body, but they didn't bother to ask any questions. I felt horrible and vulnerable. I have seen thousands of murders on TV, but seeing the murders up close unglued me. I called Randy to tell him what we saw and how we felt. He said, "Oh brother, haven't you read the fine print in Psalm 91:7?

> *A thousand may fall at your side and ten thousand at your right hand; but it will not come near to you.*
>
> (KJV 2000)

I thought "at my side" was near enough. Does this verse mean I still had another 9,996 murders to witness? Somehow his words still comforted me.

Joaquin moved his family into a home nearby and a thief tried to steal his car but Joaquin chased him away and called for the neighborhood watchman to help. The watchman asked him in which direction the thief ran. Joaquin pointed east and the watchmen walked westward. The neighborhood decided to buy the watchman a shotgun, but a week later thieves stole the shotgun. That first year was hard.

Years later, Kathy was driving the boys to church. The car in front of her stopped and a man got out brandishing a gun. He was angry and wanted to shoot somebody. Kathy stopped the car right behind him, told the boys to get down and began to shout, "In the name of Jesus, I rebuke you spirit of murder. I bind you." Suddenly, the man seemed to be startled, jumped back into his car and drove away. Don't mess with Mama Bear.

Robbery still is too much a part of life in Medellín. Some of my pastors walk around with a cheap cell phone and a phony wallet just in case they get robbed. Thieves even stole the urinals from the bathroom in church. If someone goes through all the trouble to steal urinals, I think they have earned their money. Once, when I was upset about some sound equipment stolen from the church, my friend, Jerry Manderfield, the director of Christ for the Nations of South America, said, "Hey, that is why we are here. We can't be surprised if sinners sin. We are here to bring them Jesus." Great point.

Now it was time to start the church. I had been dreaming and planning for years but I did not think about the first steps. It was like a fire escape ladder; I had it all planned out from the second floor to the top, but I did not have a clue how to start from the ground floor. I had handed out the cassette tape that painted my vision for the church, which I called Vision 2000. I talked about being a church of contagious love where everyone was a minister and multitudes would become disciples of Jesus in the river of the Holy Spirit. In the last year in Cali, Kathy and I would spend nights walking around in circles and dreaming out loud about the future church. We would stop, write a few things down and then walk around more, dreaming and dreaming. Sometimes I think the dreaming was more real than the dreams coming true. We made hundreds of copies of the Vision 2,000 tape and handed them out to anyone interested in listening to it. After each time I handed someone the tape, I thought about grabbing it back because it did not seem possible to reach 2000 in a thousand years, let alone by 2000.

Since Colombia was playing the United States in the World Cup, we decided to invite the neighbors over to watch the match with the plan to talk about Jesus at halftime. Write this down as the number one way *not* to start a church. First of all, the neighbors showed up with bottles of booze; and secondly, the United States won the game on the auto goal of Andrés Escobar. A week later, Andrés was gunned down outside a nightclub just a few miles from our home. Some of the mafia had put money into the game and took revenge on Andrés for the loss.

So, we tried again. We started a Thursday night Bible study and invited everyone we met. I was just as nervous that night as when our sons were born. I knew this was either the beginning of something huge or the end of nothing. Five people showed up. Over the first month, the group grew to eight. One always came drunk, another was dying of cancer and a third pulled me back into the kitchen to ask me if I expected him to be sexually faithful to his wife. He had almost twenty *amantes* (lovers) and told me I was crazy to expect him to give up all those women. I told him to look at the owner's manual, the Bible, and give it a try. He came back a month later beaming with pride, "Pastor, I now am sleeping only with my wife and two others." This city would be harder than I thought.

The drunk sobered up and fell in love with the Holy Spirit. The lady with cancer was healed and shocked the doctors, and eventually the man with the lovers became a man faithful to one wife. We grew in the next months to about twenty-five people and found a small room to rent near the Unicentro. We bought thirty chairs and set them up with the sound equipment. We did not have a worship leader so I had to torture the people with a few songs before the preaching part, my comfort zone. Twenty-six people attended that first Sunday; the offering was 7,000 pesos (about $5). Kathy had put in 4,000 pesos. That got me wondering how we were going to support this church in the long run. So far we were using our savings and some donations from the States to pay for the church.

As the drunks, the adulterers and the sick continued to come, Jesus changed them into lovers of God. Soon we had about eighty people. We rented the multi-purpose room in the Unicentro, with a capacity of 120. We continued to grow there until one day the Holy Spirit showed up with power. Our friends Edgar and Liz de Castillo helped us minister that Sunday and people fell to the floor and suddenly began to speak, rather scream, tongues. We were not ready for this. One big fellow was screaming in tongues and I was concerned the police would come. Two old ladies fell on the floor without anyone catching them. When I looked down at one of them, I saw blood on the floor and thought I had killed her. I thought, "I had come to Medellín to heal, and now there are two dead ladies on the floor." I felt sick in my stomach and bent down to see how they were. They were marvelous, swimming in the Spirit, happy as a fish in water. One did cut her elbow a little when she fell, but she did not feel a thing.

The next day the administration called us to let me know they were kicking us out because we were not Catholic, and crazy. I almost agreed with them. But I was also angry. It was the first time in my life I experienced prejudice. As a white man from the United States, I had never felt any prejudice, except from cowboys when I had hair down to my waist.

The next day we rented the movie theater in the same Unicentro. The lesson: A kick in the butt helps you go forward. We started in the movie theater with about a hundred people and grew quickly. But one Sunday fell on Christmas day and only fifty people showed up. In Colombia, the attendance goes down on Christmas and Easter, unlike in the United States. I went home angry and depressed, thinking I had risked everything for a church of fifty people. I wanted to take all the Vision 2000 cassettes back. Then, I remembered the microphone stand and said, "Lord, I will be a good pastor to these fifty, or just five people." I have learned the hardest person to pastor is me.

One night I was preparing a sermon about Jesus' promise to see His glory, while Kathy was in her room praying to see His glory. Praying is better than preparing sermons—the glory came down on Kathy. She said she could hardly bear the weight of His presence. Though I did not experience what she did, we both sensed something greater was coming for the church. The meetings were growing in freedom; the people were becoming more conscious of God than themselves, raising their hands and beaming with joy. The people were actually enjoying the worship instead of looking constipated. Finally, church was a place we loved being.

The owner of the theater told us he received a bomb threat because of our church services. Again, they said they were going to "echar polvera." This time I knew what it meant. We had to suspend the meeting for one week, but the owner decided to let us continue. It's a good thing that people who make these threats are also liars; nothing came of it.

God began to send us quality people with a desire to work for the vision God had for the city. Several had had dreams of two gringo pastors coming to Medellín; when they arrived at the meeting, they knew they were called to help us. Lucho, Juan David and Aldolfo have been with us for twenty years and are strong, loving pastors. Kathy and I are amazed by the quality of people God has given this ministry. We have gone through hell, heaven and high waters together, but we have come through with a seasoned friendship and a great visionary team. Each pastor on the team has one eye on the church and the other eye on the city. I tell them they are pastors of all of Medellín, whether the people know it or not.

A good friend, Jerry Anderson, President of La Red, told me about a pastor who challenged a businessman to take the millions of dollars he had stashed in the local bank and invest it in the kingdom of God for his city. His business responded to the challenge and invested into his community. A year later he called the pastor to tell him he had a word for him, too. Maybe the pastor thought he was going to donate to his church, but he said, "Pastor, as you challenged me to take my money closed up in a bank and invest it in our city, God wants you to take your ministry closed inside your church and invest it in the city." From that moment, the pastor shifted his ministry's focus and is now making a huge impact in his city. Our pastors have the same focus: the church exists to exalt Jesus and transform the city. Lucho and his wife, Luz V, lead marriage seminars in churches and companies all over the country. Juan David always has a crusade going, or is speaking on a secular TV program, or is ministering to the employees of a business. When Adolfo visits one church member in the hospital, he prays for twenty other people, and miracles happen.

But it was not always easy to establish unity in the church. In the first years we raised up leaders who came and left—and sometimes slammed the door on their way out. One dear couple began to follow the teachings of a cult-like church and were convinced that we were not deep or holy enough. Several people left the church after pastors who promised a holier and deeper walk, but usually once they arrived at said holy church, it was not holy enough. Then they formed a holier church that was not holy enough either, and the spiral went on and on. But this one couple in particular left with pieces of our heart and they drew about twenty other leaders with them. I felt so vulnerable following that loss that I did not want to answer the phone for fear that someone else was saying goodbye. Church hurts are some of the worst hurts because we open our souls and our dreams in those relationships.

It hurt to hear the false accusations against us, but God showed me Numbers 16 and 17, where Korah led a rebellion against Moses and Aaron. God told them to gather the rods of all the leaders of the tribes, write their initials on each one and leave them overnight in the tabernacle. The rod that God chose would blossom with flowers and fruit. God was saying I was not to use my little rod of authority to clobber people over the head, but rather, I was to lay my authority down. I was not to justify myself, nor speak against those who were criticizing me. If God was not giving us the authority to win Medellín, then I could go to Florida and be a fishing guide or a writer. It was hard staying quiet because the cult began to threaten us with lawsuits, but I let God take our case. After a short season in the darkness of the secret place, God slowly vindicated us with a new confidence, a fresh love and more growth. I think there is a fresh anointing that only comes from attacks and criticism. There is a deeper love that only comes from forgiving. After about a month, God brought a new confidence and growth to our church and better yet, our authority was soaked in love, not anger. We only have authority over what we deeply love. True authority comes from a love that is willing to die.

During this time, Randy wrote me the following letter:

Dear Andrew,

Your letter touched my heart. I know the pain is like salt in a wound. We don't know that we have a soul until it hurts.

Pray according to the law of restitution in the Old Testament where God commands what was stolen from us will come back five times. It channels the power of pain, making your tears for the latter rain that is coming to your church. It seems clear that God can never use a man powerfully until He has hurt him deeply, so as to protect him so he will never touch His glory. In this case, you are the man.

Maybe you asked, "Why?!" The answer is that God already swore by Himself that no man can touch His glory and live. Therefore, it is necessary that God breaks our hearts to protect us from greatly exalting ourselves, beyond the measure of glory that we can take. In our secret hidden innermost heart we can exalt ourselves, but God is passing us through the purifying fire to get us safely to a much higher level, a higher dimension and magnitude of ministry which would make an ordinary man intoxicated with pride and self-exaltation.

Stand firm. Grab the helm. Trust God and prepare for the harvest of souls greater than you can imagine!

I love you,

Randy

As we grew to more than five hundred people in the movie theatre, we had to start a second meeting in a wedding hall nearby. I would say, "Amen" at the end of the service in the theatre and run to catch a taxi to say, "Hello" in the wedding hall. Then God gave us faith to believe for a bigger place. I would tell the people we were going to have a super warehouse. Kathy and I started to look for the super warehouse, wearing out a few realtors. The very first warehouse was well located, spacious and perfect, but the price was more than double our budget, so we looked at another sixty warehouses. While I was traveling during this time, Kathy and Jesus were having a real sit-down. Jesus asked her, "Which warehouse do you want?" She said the first one. Jesus said, "Go for it." When I arrived home, Kathy had a grin and a shine on her face that made me think she was pregnant, but she told me God wanted us to have the first warehouse. I did not think it was probable, but on her faith, I called the owner and he let us rent it for half the price for the first six months, after which time he would raise the price forty per cent. We had to grow or die. So, with five hundred people, we started meetings in the hot, greasy-floored warehouse that could seat a thousand. Since then we have added more warehouses to seat more than two thousand, with more auditoriums for the children, office and leadership institute. The warehouse used to be a car repair center; now it was repairing people.

SEVENTEEN

The Safest Place on Earth

I read about a couple who was worn thin by the worldwide wars and decided to investigate contemporary history to find the safest place on earth to live. Finally they found their paradise, packed their belongings and moved to their archipelago of refuge. They wrote to their families that they had found security and bliss in the chain of islands off the coast of Argentina. The year was 1981, right before the British invaded the Falkland Islands.

Kathy and I decided the safest place in the world is in the center of God's will, right in the middle of Medellín. We were right: so far we do not have any extra holes in our bodies from knife or bullet wounds. We have been robbed and threatened, but never harmed. I once ana-lyzed how many people were killed violently per year in Medellín and figured that if the four of us lived there for twenty-five years, the statistical chances of one of us being killed would be about for-ty-five percent. But I believed we were safe. Nevertheless, there are more martyrs today being tortured and killed for the cause of Christ than ever. In two millennia of Christian history, about 70 million faithfuls have given their lives for the faith, and of these, 45.5 million, a full sixty-five percent, lived in the last century, according to Anto-nio Socci in his book *I Nuovi Perseguitati (The New Persecuted)*. So following Jesus is not that safe.

Jesus told His men to get in the boat and consequently, right smack in the center of a huge, black storm. The waves were over their heads and the wind was over their voices. So much for being "safe" in His will. But Jesus had peace in the storm. He stood up and threw that peace like a mantle over the storm. That tells me if I want to have authority over a storm, I must first have peace inside the storm. I always thought of peace as being a quiet nice sort of fellow, but Jesus shows us that peace is really like a tough guy who quiets the noisy bar just by walking in the room. In the center of God's will, Jesus slowly stands up inside us and the waves calm down. Jesus has power over all storms because He first has peace in all storms.

When we arrived in Medellín, it was the number one city for murders in this hemisphere and it was also the least churched (Protestant) per capita. A man once came to the office with a gun asking for me, but the secretary said I was not there, so he left. She lied. Another time, some known killers were circling our church on a motorcycle, but a little lady who ran a soda shack nearby the church reported them to the police. Within minutes, they were arrested. This sweet lady, Arcelia, has become a great home group leader. Twice she led over fifty people to the Lord during funeral services.

The church has been robbed several times and threatened a few times with bombs, but no one has ever been wounded on the grounds. We did have one young man's arm stabbed during an outdoor crusade and to this day, his arm hangs limp to his side, but his faith is firm. At a nearby church, a thief threw gasoline on the night watchman, and with a lit match, demanded the keys to the money room. Thieves play hardball here.

Don't Do It

About ten years ago, God interrupted my preaching when I was talking about healing, and a dear man, Juan Manuel, felt led to walk over to a man in a wheelchair and pray for him. The man felt the heat of God run through his legs and he stood up, the first time in three years. His wife was shocked and everyone around began to gasp and applaud. I was trying to get to my next point about healing, but I never did. We listened to his testimony and started to pray for the sick and many were healed. God's sermons are better than mine.

Just recently, I don't remember what I was preaching about, but I sensed God was interrupting me from the inside. I stopped for a few seconds looking around the auditorium and announced, "Someone here is about to do something very wicked this afternoon. In the name of Jesus, don't do it." Everyone looked at me as I wondered what to do next. I went on with the sermon and gave the invitation to receive Christ. Among the fifty people at the altar, I remember one man crying uncontrollably. I did not think too much about him because it is a common sight, but after the service, the ushers brought me a man named Jairo, who wanted to talk to me.

Jairo was planning to pick up a gun around 2 p.m. and kill a businessman. The day before, a youth in our church invited Jairo to come to the Saturday 4 p.m. service. Jairo blew him off. The youth returned an hour later and begged him to come to the 6 p.m. service and Jairo said he was too busy. The youth would not let it go. He woke up early Sunday morning and knocked on Jairo's door to take him to the early 8 a.m. service and of course, Jairo said he had some important business to attend to. An hour later, the youth was back begging him to come to the 10 a.m. service. Jairo finally decided to come, thinking he could kill some time before doing the actual killing. In the service, Jairo did not pay attention to a word; he was plotting his hit. Suddenly, he heard the words, "Someone is going to do something wicked…" He said it felt like somebody punched him in the chest. When I gave the invitation, he ran to the altar.

The next day, as I was walking outside our church, Jairo came up and asked me if I remembered him. He was attending the new believers' class. When I told him I sure did remember him, he said, "Look Pastor what I have," and reached into his jacket. I flinched but he only pulled out a big Bible. "Do you know what this is? This is my new weapon." I went home thinking some businessman was alive tonight and didn't even know it was Jesus who saved him.

Once I took the pastoral team to San Andres Island for a time of rest and planning. We rented a golf cart to putt around the island. Two of the pastors were following behind us in a taxi as I was driving the cart with Pastor Juan David at my side. We were enjoying the peace and calm of the Caribbean night. I said to Juan it would be nice to live there and plant a church since San Andres is the safest place in Colombia. At that very instant, two men with guns on a motorcycle came up behind us to rob us. I did not even notice them, but the taxi driver behind us did. He honked and blinked his lights, frightening off the thieves. I turned just in time to see the motorcycle rush by and wondered why the taxi driver was making such a fuss. In the very moment I thought I was in a safe place, someone had been aiming a gun at me. It's not what we see that should color our perception of safety, but what God sees.

Don't get me wrong, I really enjoy being alive. I would like to live another hundred years. George Burns said he couldn't wait till he reached one hundred because not many people die at that age. One thing is for sure, we are not really living until we are ready to die. Jonathan Edwards, the great theologian of the First Great Awakening, said we are like a spider on a thread hanging over a fire. What holds us back from falling into eternity is a thin, silver wire. This earth is only safe if we know what we are falling into when it snaps. As Ecclesiastes 12:6 says, "Yes, remember your Creator now while you are young, before the silver cord of life snaps." (NLT) When we know we are always close to snapping, life is richer. It is like riding on a cable car over the mountains and you notice how thin the cable is. You feel afraid and yet so alive and the mountains pulse with life. Living may be dangerous to our health, but the thrill is healthy. About 275,000 people die everyday and the average person lives about 24,150 days. The Psalmist asked for a heart of wisdom to be able to count his days, which means I think, to cherish everyday. We will only see the sun set so many times. We will only have so many conversations at the kitchen table. We will only catch so many fish. But we think we have forever. And we will, in one place or another.

Medellín was also the leading kidnapping city in this hemisphere. I think a kidnapping is harder for the families than for the victims, because as least the victims know what is going on. The families put their lives on hold, holding their breath each time the phone rings. I had lunch with a man kidnapped and held captive for seven years by the FARC guerillas. Most of his clothes rotted off him. When the Colombian army rescued him, he said the ride home on the helicopter was gorgeous. The whole day was heaven: hugging his family, taking a hot shower, putting on clean socks, walking around his house and crawling into bed with his wife. What once was just background routine to his busy political life, was now his life and paradise. He said he survived by looking at each of his captors and deeply forgiving them every day. Recently I had dinner with a businessman who was also kidnapped by the FARC and held hostage for six months. Ever since his release he has enjoyed his life deeply. Clean clothes, his wife's voice, hot coffee and books are all miracles to him.

We love the rescue stories of miners, castaways, mountain climbers and prisoners. *Proof of Life* with Russell Crowe is one of my favorite movies. Somehow we feel the glory of their homecoming. When the families reunite, the food is served and the prison clothes come off, we think there must be a homecoming for us, too. In this moment, we are free. We are not kidnapped, lost or imprisoned; so why don't we enjoy our freedom and the few people who love us? When we hear a good rescue story, we are surprised by the sudden welling-up of tears, which seem to have come from a place we forgot was there. We have not been trapped in a mine or tortured in the jungle, but the greater the rescue, the more we feel it is somehow our story, too. And in a way, it is. We were all rescued from nothingness when we were conceived. In a way, each morning we wake up, we have been rescued. Every day should be a celebration of our rescue. We can go to the bathroom, get dressed, pet the dog, make coffee and walk out the door anytime we please. Maybe we should yell, "Freedom!" as we roll out the driveway.

For years I refused to listen to the story of Jesus rescuing me. I had no idea what I needed rescuing from. Forgiven for what? On the day I asked for His forgiveness, I was airlifted out of despair, but still, some days I wake up feeling average. I am not overcome with the sheer joy of hot tea. I have freedom to plan the day and turn on music, but I need a class in gratitude. I need to keep on hearing the rescue stories until I am dizzy with the delight of clean socks. G.K. Chesterton wrote, "If my children wake up Christmas morning and have somebody to thank for putting candy in their stockings, have I no one to thank for putting two feet into mine?" God pulled us out of nothingness. In a way, we are on a helicopter on the way home and clean socks are stacked in the dresser for the rest of our lives.

EIGHTEEN

Fresh Wind of Revival

Near the end of our first year in Medellín, I was listening on the Internet to an interview by a Vero Beach radio station with Randy Clark about what God was doing in Toronto, Canada. Randy shared how the power of God touched his life when Rodney Howard-Browne prayed for him and how later he went to a small church in Toronto for a three-day revival. This little revival exploded into the ongoing revival impacting more than 20,000 Christian leaders all over the world. Since then, John and Carol Arnott have become our friends. They are the most down to earth, loving people we know, yet what God is doing there is highly controversial. The Toronto Blessing is known for its transferable anointing with visible forms of outbreaks of laughter, weeping, groaning, shaking, falling, "drunkenness" and even behaviors that have been described as a "cross between a jungle and a farmyard." Of greater significance, however, are the changed lives. It's all about the fruit.

During the Randy Clark interview, the soundman at the radio station fell to the floor. Then the interviewer and the other two workers fell down under the power of God. Randy was left alone at the microphone, and eventually, had to leave for his next appointment. For thirty minutes the airwaves were soundless. Finally, the interviewer crawled to the microphone, saying God was doing something unexplainable and wonderful. Then he was on the floor again.

People began driving over to the station, which is connected to the Assembly of God Church pastored by Buddy Tipton. Some people said they were not even listening to the radio but were pulled into the parking lot by the Holy Spirit. No one was praying for anyone, but as soon as the people entered the station, they fell on the floor. Soon, the corridors were full of bodies and the church sanctuary began to fill up with people worshipping, praying and falling. This was a new phenomenon for all these folks. Several pastors joined together and continued the meetings. People were repenting and talking about the changes God was making in their lives. After about a week, the palpable presence of the Spirit just seemed to lift and life slowly went back to normal, but in some, it left lasting change.

As I was listening to this report, I decided to fly to Vero Beach and see the exact place where this happened. A month later, I drove up to the station and ran into the office to ask the manager, "Is this where the revival happened?" He said yes. I asked him where it went, but he didn't know. He said he'd never seen anything like it but it just ended. I talked to Pastor Buddy and he also did not know why it ended, but he said it was something.

While visiting Kathy's parents in New Jersey, I heard Randy Clark was ministering in a church in Harrisburg, Pennsylvania. I drove three hours, three nights in a row in the sleet because I was so hungry for something more. The first night I sat in the back next to a portly lady who was laughing and jerking, asking me if I thought it was wonderful. She annoyed me because in my pride I thought God would want to touch a missionary before touching a giddy lady. I was feeling nothing. I looked around to see about half of the people touched emotionally. I was used to preachers working people into an emotional lather, but Randy was talking as calmly as a banker explaining interest rates. As I listened to him share about his experiences with the fire of God, my hunger grew. On the third night, I drove my wife and kids with me and I went up for prayer and confessed every secret sin I could think of. Gradually, the weight of

God's presence fell on me. The word for glory in the Hebrew is *Kabod*, which means *weight*. I was getting *kabodded*. I did not feel electricity or fire, but I did feel a heavy blanket over my body.

Almost a year later, we returned to the States to go to Rodney Howard Browne's meetings in the Tampa Sun Dome. On the platform, some pastors and well-known singers were trying to give their testimonies but were not able to finish. Some fell over and others laughed uncontrollably. I was not sure what to make of it all. Rodney called all the pastors to come down to the main floor to lay hands on us. I fell on the floor and wondered what I was doing there. I did sense an invisible blanket over me, a little like the Harrisburg experience, so I stayed still, listening. Suddenly I felt my heart melted with love for Jesus. I must have been there for almost an hour, while our friends waited for us to go to lunch. I felt light and free for days.

When I returned to Medellín, I was afraid I would not be able to carry back the fresh anointing to the church. The South American Indians take the burning coals from their campfire and wrap them inside big leaves, carrying them to their next site. Once they arrive at their new camp, they blow on the coals to ignite the fire. I saw I needed to carry the fresh fire in the leaves of the Word of God. I needed to see where my experiences lined up with the Word of God and then, once in Medellín, I'd open the Word, share my experience and fan the flame. Once, I had tried to bring back the fire without explaining it with the Word. When I came back from Argentina where Claudio Freidzon prayed for me, I rushed home to impart the fresh anointing to Kathy. Upon arriving, I dropped the suitcases and after the hello kiss, asked Kathy to close her eyes as I laid hands on her. I prayed for the fire to fall. Nothing happened. She said, "Now what?" I said I didn't know and we just laughed.

However, when I returned from Tampa, something did happen. The pastors were hungry for more of the Holy Spirit. I shared the Scriptures about how fire falling on unbelievers in the Old Testament brought judgment, while the fire falling on believers brought cleansing and power. As I prayed for them, the room filled with brightness. The blanket was now on them, too. Then, Kathy and I took our pastoral team to the meetings of Ricardo Rodriquez in Bogota. We would return to the hotel drunk in the Spirit, in love with Jesus and each other. We also found a new boldness to share Christ and pray for the sick. If it were not for this fresh anointing and freedom, I don't think we would have made it in Medellín.

Heidi

I had no idea that heaven would leak through the cracks when I pushed in the VHS tape to watch a teaching by Dr. Heidi Baker. Heidi and her husband Roland are missionaries to Mozambique. Strangely, she was a very happy missionary. Some think she is a cracked pot, but eternity breaks through the cracks in the pot. Paul talks about our life being fragile clay pots and the treasure of His glory seeps through (2 Corinthians 4:7). Kathy and I watched the video of the blond woman burn and burn in heaven's fire.

I have enjoyed the wonderful ministry gifts of many people but this was different. Admiring people move in their gifts is much like the admiration I have for the kids who juggle torches of fire at the traffic lights in Medellín. They juggle the fire and then take an offering, a lot like church. But watching Heidi, we knew we were not watching a fire juggler but a little lady doused in fire, and yet, kept burning in joy. We knew this was something for us. God was talking out of a burning bush again. I had tried to imitate the ministry gifts of others, usually burning myself in the process, but Heidi opened up a door of hope and wonder. We thought, *Hey, we can't juggle, but we can fall in love and burn.*

It was like hearing about a new land where the fruit grows tall in one day and the flowers bloom each hour. Could there really be a place where the blue sky is so close and real that you could touch it and make it swirl like water, and where the brightly colored fish in the streams swim near the surface and are never shy? We were hearing about blind ladies being healed, their eyes swirling with life, and about abused and tortured children becoming innocent and brave again. She was talking about Mozambique, where children die in the streets, the government is cruel and everything is stolen, but she also spoke of the beauty of heaven coming close to earth. She spoke of miracles and the multitudes running to Jesus. This excited me. Heidi drew back the curtains for us to see the colors of heaven.

So I decided I had to talk to this lady. In 2005, I traveled with my oldest son, Andrew Michael, to the Toronto Airport church where Heidi was one of the guest speakers. We arrived a day earlier. When we entered the church, only a handful of people lay on the floor "soaking" as someone played on the keyboard. They told us the conference did not start until the next day and invited us to soak on the floor. At first I thought, *we did not travel 3,000 miles to lie on the ground.* I could stay and soak in Colombia where the ground is warmer. However, we stayed and soaked for a couple of hours while I looked up at the ceiling wondering if I was wasting my time. Slowly I felt God softening my heart and showing me my pride and sense of entitlement.

The next day the place was packed, but I was determined to speak to Heidi. I wanted to ask her the secret of raising and training the pastors for the 7,000 churches she had planted at the time. I was determined to take her secret strategy back to South America. I knew Heidi was the speaker on the second night, so I was rubbernecking to see if she had arrived. I noticed some lady was weeping and laughing, sprawled out and blocking the steps up to the platform. I thought someone needed to deal with this disturbed lady because she was blocking the stairs for Heidi. When that lady finally got up and wobbled to the pulpit, I figured out it was Heidi. But before she could utter a word, she was down again and lost in Jesus. I was waiting to hear some church growth secrets, something I could pack up and take home, but I had to stand and watch the fire burn. I was frustrated, but finally, I took off my shoes. I realized I was standing on holy ground.

Still, I was determined to ask Heidi some questions about church planting. Somehow we were invited to have lunch with Heidi and a few others. I had my chance! When we arrived at the restaurant, I was trying to get her attention to talk about my important stuff, but she was too busy ministering love to the waitress. The waitress sobbed away in Heidi's arm while I was waiting to order food and ask my important questions. I got my first revival lesson. Love the person right in front of you.

When I finally got to ask Heidi how she and Rolland planted so many churches, Heidi slowly turned her head to me, her eyes still red from crying, and said, as if to pity me, "O Andrew, Jesus will tell you," and then went back to deal with the important issues of peoples' hearts. At first I was offended, I had paid all the expenses, put plans on hold, and knocked myself out to get to Toronto, only to hear, "Jesus will tell you." I ate my lunch, a little stunned. Later I got to thinking maybe Heidi meant that Jesus was going to show up with a huge chalkboard and give me a detailed plan of church planting. However, Jesus did not say, "Come to Me and think," but "Come to Me and drink." As I learned how to come into His presence more and more to drink, Jesus began to lead us to plant one church after another. And it is accelerating. He really is telling us, step by step, how to plant more and healthier churches.

In January 2009, Heidi came to our church in Medellín for three days. The meetings were wonderful. The love and humility of Jesus conquered our hearts, many were saved and healed, but the greatest impact of Heidi's visit was behind the scenes. God wants the best room to be the back room. Kathy and I loved her ministry, but how she dealt with bad news, exhausting schedules and upset travel plans changed us forever.

Before arriving to Colombia, Heidi had had a grueling travel and ministry schedule. Also, her dear friend, Jill Austin, had died days before. Though she wanted to be at her friend's funeral, she kept her commitment to come to Colombia. She traveled alone because her assistant stayed to be at Jill's funeral. While she was in the Miami airport waiting to board the flight to Colombia, she received some very hard news about her husband being sick unto death. She then flew to Colombia, but to the wrong city. Instead of flying to Medellín where we were waiting with a bus full of youth with balloons, flowers and welcome signs, she flew to Cali where nobody was waiting for her. After frantically trying to find out what happened to Heidi, I finally managed to get Heidi's cell number and called her. She answered full of joy. She was just sitting alone on top of her suitcase worshipping Jesus without a clue of what to do. I told her she had arrived at the right country but at the wrong city. She just laughed. That floored me. I have been chewed out by tired, grumpy guest speakers when plans go wrong. She had to sleep over in a rundown hotel and take the red eye, arriving just in time for the first meeting. She was worn out, yet full of the love of Christ. At the end of the meetings, it was hard to pull her away from the children, from the hurting and the hungry. She never complained. Kathy and I just watched the fire burn and burn and burn.

Charles and Anne Stock, pastors of Life Center in Harrisburg, Pennsylvania, came to our church after an extended fast in 1999. Before the evening meeting, they prayed for our pastoral team, and the Spirit touched each one visibly. Some cried, some laughed and some fell to the floor. When they prayed for me, nothing happened. I thought it was for the better because I had to get things going for the evening meeting. At that time, I thought I had to worry about everything and do everything in the church. I could not enjoy worship because I would worry about the ushers greeting the visitors or wonder why someone did not turn on the ceiling fans. As I got up to leave, I fell down. I did not feel anything emotional or physical. I simply fell down with my left cheek on the rug. I tried to get up but I could not. Gradually, I felt as if there was a hand holding my head against the rug. I knew Jesus was asking me a simple question, "Whose church is it? I did not hear you. Whose church is it?" And I was responding, "It is your church, Jesus. It is your church." The verse Colossians 1:18 that says Jesus is the Head of the church is not poetry. After about forty minutes I stood up, a rug burn on my cheek. Anne pointed her finger in my face to say Jesus was not finished with me. I thought He was, and I had just taken a few steps toward the auditorium when I fell down again. This time the floodgates of my heart burst open. I cried as His healing love washed over my wounded heart. I was wounded from thinking it was my church and taking people's departures personally. I was hurting and tired because I thought I had to make the church go. And now I was weeping at the feet of the real Head of the church, Jesus Christ. Years later, a little boy asked me if I was the boss of the church. I said Jesus was the boss. And he said, but you are the boss here, right? And I said, "Jesus is the boss here, really." I would like to say from that moment on I never stressed out, or took myself too seriously as pastor, but I constantly have to be reminded of His headship and His hand on my head.

Kathy and I started to attend Rodney Howard Browne's meetings and saw other pastors radically rewired and empowered by the Spirit. Rodney would call out several people with prophetic words, but he always seemed to pass me over. I wanted to put on a bright tie, but I didn't. One morning, Rodney went to play golf and left his wife to teach in the morning meeting. I was a little offended; I had spent money to be there and he was out playing golf. I almost stayed in my room to rest but as soon as Adonica started to speak, the nearness of Jesus was overpowering. I was on the first row, on the floor, weeping and crying. My heart was liquid wax. I could not stop my high pitched sobs or my hot tears. I was afraid to open my eyes for the fear of seeing Jesus or an angel. For more than an hour I trembled, snot running out of my nose. The two pastors on each side of me were also getting hammered. As Adonica, who was not bothered by us at all, finished her talk, I managed to sit back up on the chair and recompose myself until she said, "I hoped this blessed someone today." And that did it. I was on the floor laughing and crying all over again. Later on she was lifting us up and laying her hands on each one and I staggered, trying to stand still. Suddenly, I felt someone push me hard on my right shoulder blade. I stumbled forward and was upset that someone was so rude to push me in such a holy moment. When I turned around, no one was there. Why would God do that? I'm not sure, but I can say I have been more aware and expectant of the supernatural since that day. What seems scandalous and mere emotionalism has helped us be more open to the presence of God, without which we would not have survived the years to come in Colombia. The fruit of it all was falling more in love with Jesus and being able to get through the hard times without bitterness.

A year later we attended another minister's conference with Rodney, and near the end, I was thinking, "Oh well, another great conference, but no prophetic word for me." Right then he pointed to me and called Kathy and me forward, saying, "The Lord says, dig a hole and I will fill it. I see your church growing to 10,000, to 20,000, to 30,000..." (I was thinking I didn't want a church so big because I would never have time to fish!) Rodney continued, "...to 40,000 and to 50,000." I did feel the love for Medellín burn in my heart as he was praying for me, but I considered his prophecy was a little inflated. A week later, I called an Episcopal priest, Father Bud, who knew Rodney well. Bud was touched by the fire of God and wrote a great book with a great title, "Fire in a Wax Museum." I asked Bud if Rodney was known for giving inflated, exaggerated prophecies and he said, "Andrew, he seems to be very precise. If I were you, I would prick up my ears to his words."

So I carried the prophecy of 50,000 in my heart back to Medellín, and vowed not to share it with anyone. However, a month later, I was rather excited during my preaching, maybe a little drunk on the new wine, and I blurted out the prophecy of 50,000. Unfortunately, everyone seemed to believe it. People would say to each other that our church would grow to 50,000. I felt like I did about the tape declaring 2,000 people by the year 2000. (By the way, we did make it to 2,300 by the year 2000 but are still a long way from 50,000.)

Two months later, a medical doctor from Washington who moved in prophecy, visited our church. After a week, she said, "Andrew, since the first day I have been here, I saw something written on your forehead. Can I tell you?" I was not sure I wanted to hear, but said to go ahead. She said it was the number 50,000. Today, our church has more than 12,000, if you include our church plants. I am still slow of heart to believe. But I will dig a hole and maybe fall in. I just know Jesus wants to conquer Medellín in love.

NINETEEN

Bullrings and Rat Fishing

In 2002 Kathy took her intercession team to pray around the city's bullring, walking around human excrement, broken bottles and who knows what. She also put a photo on the refrigerator door of the bullring. Most people have family photos on the fridge; we have bullring photos. She even dared to pray that the city would fix the place up and put a roof on it so we could have some church meetings there. And of course in 2003, the city fixed the place up, redid the bathrooms and put a roof on that closed and opened electronically. God answers beyond what we ask. I told the pastors we should rent the city's bullring for a meeting. They thought I was hearing from God, but for me, it was just was an idea. We started to plan a Sunday morning meeting in the bullring and I knew what I was going to preach:

Not by the blood of bulls but by the blood of the Lamb of God.
HEBREWS 10:4 *(Author's paraphrase)*

We encouraged the church to invite their friends and enemies to the meeting. We rented forty-five buses to bring the people from the remote neighborhoods, and prayed hard. The week before the event, I was alone at home. Suddenly I felt overcome by dread and insecurity. A dark voice accused me in my mind, saying, "Who do you think you are to have these mass meetings?" I could envision the place almost empty. The bullring can hold up 15,000, so empty would feel really empty. Then I had another image of the place being full. That scared me even more. The darkness was ridiculing me and I started agreeing, "I am no Billy Graham. This is a set up for a huge failure." It is fine to have such thoughts, but the trouble starts when we agree with the thoughts—and I was agreeing with them. So, I tried to think how to get out of the meeting, but the word had already been spread over the whole city.

One morning, alone in my room and still in my pajamas, I opened my computer and punched in *daystar.com*, which streams live Christian programming. I have no idea why I did. I was never able to connect to Daystar before, but that day I connected instantly. Pastor David Demola was preaching about faith. I had met Pastor Demola a few times in New Jersey years before, so it was nice to see someone I knew online. He has a huge, wonderful church; I doubted he would remember me. On the broadcast, he said, "God doesn't look at the appearance of a man, but He looks at the faith in his heart." I thought that was pretty good preaching. That connected with me. Then he floored me, saying:

> *Eighteen years ago I remember talking to a young pastor, Andrew McMillan, who told me about his vision to go to Colombia. Looking at him, I thought to myself, "Poor fellow, Colombia is going to stomp on him, chew him up and spit him out. But you should hear what God is doing in Colombia through his ministry!"*

I gasped, "What? How? Is this real? Did I really hear that? What are the chances?" Dr. Demola went to his next point, but I was on the floor. How did I happen to connect to this preaching at the very moment where he was talking about me, whom he hardly knew? I realized that God was confirming the bullring and I celebrated by walking around the room like a kid out of school. Then after five minutes, I stopped and asked. "Hey. What did he mean by "looking at him"? Did I look like a wimp?

Sunday morning was a beautiful day, but the anxiety was

churning inside me. When we got to the bullring, the people were arriving in the rented buses. Everyone was excited and happy. I might have been the only person worried. More than 10,000 people raised their voices to the opening song, "Open the Floodgates of Heaven." At that instant, they opened the electronic roof and we let loose dozens of doves. Most of the people did not know the roof was electronic; they were pretty amazed to see their praise open the heavens.

We have had fifteen meetings in the bullring with attendance up to 10,000 people. Once we conservatively estimated a thousand people at the altar call for salvation. We also had some great dramatic presentations. We had a young woman dressed as an angel come down a cable from 80 feet above to the floor. (No man would volunteer to be the angel!) We have had horses, torches, doves, celebrities and fireworks. The drama and communications teams are so creative that I just get out of the way.

In one meeting there, a man who had not walked in ten years stood up from his wheelchair, which ignited the atmosphere for many healings. After the meeting, I was hanging around praying with Kathy for the sick. Only a few hundred remained. Two ladies brought their friend who had been blind for three years. I was tired and just wanted to go home and watch some football, but I prayed for her. When she fell down screaming, I thought, *O great. I got a live one here.* They picked her up and I asked her what was happening; she said nothing. I prayed again. She screamed and fell down again. They picked her up and she looked around and screamed again, saying, "Yo puedo ver!" (I can see!) I asked, "Are you sure?" I was just as shocked as she was. I even asked her friends if she was really blind before, I mean, completely blind. I was just like the Pharisees in John 9 who tried to find a logical explanation for the healing of the blind man. She came back to give her testimony the next week, but I forgot to get her name and number. I now know I need to be a faithful scribe and get the testimonies written down with the facts. Bill Johnson, pastor of the Bethel Church in Redding, CA, said we need to be faithful stewards over the testimonies because if we are faithful over a little, God will give us bigger and better miracles to steward. Who wouldn't want that?

Well, lots of people are uncomfortable with miracles because they put a demand on our life. Jesus says we are more responsible before God when we see miracles. He did not pull any punches when He said,

> Then began he to upbraid the cities wherein most of his mighty works were done, because they repented not: Woe unto thee, Chorazin! woe unto thee, Bethsaida! for if the mighty works, which were done in you, had been done in Tyre and Sidon, they would have repented long ago in sackcloth and ashes. But I say unto you, It shall be more tolerable for Tyre and Sidon at the day of judgment, than for you.
>
> MATTHEW 11:20–22 (KJV)

If Jesus heals my body, then I know what I do with my body is important and I am accountable before Him. If we never see God invading our bodies with healing, we can get the gnostic idea that what we do in our bodies is not too important because, after all, God sees our heart. But when healing comes to town, the presence of God convicts us to see our hearts as they really are. We can be changed inside and out. The bad news is that we must change; the good news is that we can.

One of the great secrets I have learned is we feel afraid doing new things; walking by faith does not always feel peaceful. But when we do it anyway, the peace will eventually come. In the meantime, our trembling faith pleases God. Then there are other times when the boldness of heaven gives us great grace to do things without any fear. But for me, my faith walk is usually in fear and trembling.

For the ministry, it has been a dream come true to see the thousands coming to Christ in the bullring and in the church. But I have some personal dreams, too, like taking my sons marlin fishing.

Sometimes these have had to take a backseat; there are no marlins in the polluted Medellín River. I wondered why God had not put a blue ocean next to Medellín, but God has other ways of fulfilling our dreams.

Rats are part of our story in Medellín. Once a big, burly rat jumped out of the kitchen drawer towards Kathy. She screamed so loud it scared the poor rat half to death. Another time, a rat trying to get under Kathy's pillow, woke her up. These rats are fearless. I finally killed that rat with fifty rounds of a pellet gun. Another time, we had a rat in our closet. Our friend, Steven Swisher, offered to help kill it. Steve is a big strong man and now was armed with a broom, but when the rat ran out, Steve jumped up on the bed and yelled, "You didn't tell me it was a horse." Colombian rats are the Marines of the rat world.

One night I was sharing with our 700 home group leaders, when I heard several screams. At first I thought the Spirit had touched someone; stuff like that does happen here. But then I saw the whole back row, one after another jump up and scream. It was not God, but a big rat wreaking havoc. It was like a cartoon. We don't have church mice but fat, healthy rats. That night I got a great idea. I told my boys we would go rat fishing.

On Sunday night, about the only time the church "sanctuary" (three warehouses joined together) is quiet and unused, we loaded up the car with our rods, reels and chunks of chicken. We selected the smallest hooks in the box because rats have tiny mouths, which is a good thing. In the dimmed lights, we positioned ourselves in the center of the sanctuary and laid out our lines to the hole at the base of the drainage pipe. I had the rod and my sweet boys were armed with a golf club and a baseball bat. What other sport combines all the major sports? With the same excitement of seeing a sailfish's beak playing with the bait, we saw the quick shadows of two rats near the chicken. The anticipation equaled that of seeing the large swirl of a blue marlin. The first tug, almost imperceptible, placed me in that wonderful and tortuous territory where fishermen ache to yank the hook but know they must wait. Those few seconds are a swirl of pain and joy. Finally yanking and setting the hook, I felt the life trembling through the line and shooting up my arms. Life connected to life. The rat scampered, zigzagged and then bee-lined towards us faster than I could reel in the line. At that moment, I was not sure I was happy I had him hooked. I jumped up on the chair while my boys screamed, swinging their weapons with the lust of Vikings. After a minute of tangling themselves in the fishing line, and banging the cement floor over a hundred times, they finally stunned the rat and then clubbed him into eternity. You would think we just landed a blue marlin. It was sheer celebration teetering close to tribal madness.

On that dark rainy night in the rat-infested warehouse, the blood leaked out of the rat's mouth and formed a small continent on the floor. Breathing hard, we stared at each other in mutual admiration. The beauty of living speared us. My boys and I drove home on the cold, wet streets of Medellín, warmed by an inner Caribbean sunset. I know rats are disgusting and clubbing them more so. I know that the warehouse is cold and ugly. I'd rather have turquoise seas, West Virginia hills in late fall, red tailed hawks and fields of Queen Anne's lace bending to the summer breeze. I ache for the beauty of the sun sinking into a snowy forest. Beautiful places give us a glimpse of the Eden past and of heaven to come. I can imagine what William Wordsworth experienced when he wrote about London bathed in the morning light.

> *Never did sun more beautifully steep*
> *In his first splendour, valley, rock, or hill;*
> *Ne'er saw I, never felt, a calm so deep!*
> *The river glideth at his own sweet will....*

COMPOSED UPON WESTMINSTER BRIDGE,
September 3, 1802

But the wet congested streets of Medellín were no paradise. How is a warehouse with a dead rat really beautiful? I did not choose to live in Medellín for its beauty. God enflamed my heart to love the three million people, but I'd rather live in other places. It rains too much there, the traffic is brutal and it gets dark too early. Nevertheless, rat fishing in the warehouse jolted me to see the beauty of God that can flourish in any soil, at any moment. It was a flash of blue sky. My quest in life, as the ancient prophet said, is to see the beauty of the King (Isaiah 33:17). Maybe where you are right now, reading these lines, and where you are in life, is a good place for beauty to breakthrough. Your line is out and there is a swirl. If God has packed so much life and beauty into one filthy rat, how much more life can explode like a tarpon hooked on the line in our life every day?

PART SEVEN

MIRACLES

Miracles are not contrary to nature, but only contrary to what we know about nature.

—SAINT AUGUSTINE

TWENTY

Wounded Healer

Who can take away suffering without entering it?

—HENRI NOUWEN

If we had known the battles we would face, Kathy and I might not have gone to the mission field, but now we would not trade our scars for gold. The name of God's best tool for training us is trouble. Many have said, "Don't trust anyone without a limp." God wounds us like a doctor breaking a leg to reset it. He heals us so we will limp with a mercy towards other hurting people. Kathy always says, "Hurting people hurt people, but only healed people heal people." We've seen our share of common sufferings: we've said goodbye to our kids at college, we've seen our parents die, we've been sick and had problems go on and on. We have not suffered the loss of a child, but we have buried too many youth. We have been threatened but not shot or stabbed. We have seen too much blood. We have not been kidnapped, but we have cried with families waiting for news of their kidnapped sons. We have not lived on the streets, but we have felt homeless as we help people come home to the Father. In this chapter, I come close to complaining, but bear with me. In the suffering, there is healing. I do want to clarify: our suffering does not earn healing. Only the wounds of Jesus bring healing. When we hold on to past hurts, we can block the fresh river of healing. You may be healed as you read.

Stabbed in the Back

When the doctor fixed his focus on me and slowly said, "You need to have this operation," I asked him if he'd do it if he were in my place. He said yes. I asked him if he were me, would he be scared. He said yes. I said I was going to trust him, but I looked at his hands to detect any hint of tremors and then squinted at the signatures on his diplomas for any sign of forgery.

After a few bouts with the herniated disk that would pin me on the floor for four to five days at a time, I gave in to the knife. At times I could not even crawl, helpless as an upside-down, legless turtle. Going to the bathroom became an ancient, secret art.

Helplessness is the best word to describe the whole process of being driven to the hospital to make an appointment to be stabbed in the back. From the waiting room I was ushered into a small room and ordered to take off everything and put on the "forget-about-your-dignity" gown. I was led down a hallway where people were sitting on both sides while I tried to close the rear flaps. Then I mounted the gurney to be stung with the IV needle to be wheeled away by masked strangers who would flip me over like a pancake and stare at my rear for hours. At least, I thought, these were all professionals and did not know me, but at that very moment, a nurse came up and bellowed, "Pastor Andrés, I didn't know you were here!" I wondered if my butt would be on Facebook.

When the anesthesia mask was placed over my face, I was telling the nurses a joke about pastors confessing their secret sins. I think I finished the joke. I hope I finished the joke. I was gone. Almost three hours later, helpless as a calf being born, I struggled back into consciousness only wanting to hold my wife's hand and raise my hands in thanksgiving.

After a month of physical pain and enjoying the recovery at home with permitted laziness, I wondered where the pain went. Physical pain is not stored in the memory like mental or emotional pain.

When bodily pain is over, it's over, but the heart's pain does not end; it echoes a thousand times. Sometimes the memory of the inner pain is more acute than the very moment of the original wound. Sometimes the memory of a cruel word, the memory of a phone call or the memory of opening a letter is more painful than the first impact. It seems these wounds can curl into the heart and cut us deeper by turning over and over.

Enter the Cross. Jesus anguished in the emotional hell of being rejected and forgotten by the Father Himself. He became our peace— our calm over the churning waters of hurt. What has been churning for years is suddenly silenced by one word from Him who says, "I have stored my pain forever so you can go free. The knife of shame and of rejection is stuck in Me forever." Jesus is where the pain went. The only one with scars in heaven is Jesus, who says, "Look at my wounds. Touch them. They are never going away. I will keep your wounds safe in My hands so they can never hurt you again." Years ago I heard about a boy allergic to bee stings. He was in the car with his father when a bee flew inside. The boys panicked but the father trapped the bee between the roof and his hand. Then he let it go. The boy cried, "Dad, why did you do that?" The father told his son to relax and look at his hand. The stinger was in his palm and the bee could no longer hurt him.

Death has already stung Jesus, and He emerged victorious. Satan has no stinger left! Isaiah 53:5 makes it clear: "But he was pierced for our transgressions, he was crushed for our iniquities; the punishment that brought us peace was on him, and by his wounds we are healed." (NIV) So, relax and look at His hands.

When I was seven years old I was standing on the second floor porch of my grandmother's house in Halifax, Nova Scotia. It was a beautiful summer day with sailboats in the bay and tall blue spruces bending in the breeze. My mother went shopping with my grandmother and I was alone with the maid, Margaret. She was a big, quiet lady, ebony skin glistening in the sunlight. She was working in the kitchen, and I on top of the world. Everything was perfect: a bright sun, white clouds, and not a hint of suffering anywhere. Then pain pricked my leg. Then, another jolt of pain. I looked down and saw my legs covered with wasps. The pain exploded like fireworks—eighteen stings in all. Margaret hearing me scream, ran out to the porch and picked me up. She brushed off the wasps, carried me inside, stripped me naked and put me in a bath of Epsom salt. I felt strange that a lady was stripping me down, but I didn't care. I needed saving.

An hour later, my mother arrived. As she was holding me, I remember looking at Margaret sitting in a chair, quiet and in pain. In saving me, she had been stung so many times that the poison had made her sick. She hardly knew me. We hardly ever talked. But she took my pain. I remember marveling at how wonderful she was, sitting there, suffering what would have been my pain and sickness. I don't remember thanking her, perhaps I was still embarrassed she had seen me naked. I don't know if anyone thanked her. But on this sunny day, I think how good it would be to take her to lunch at a restaurant overlooking the bay. I would order her a shrimp cocktail, a piña colada and a plate of chocolates. I would plead with her to ask for everything on the menu. That would be a perfect summer day.

I owe another lady a meal, too. It was lightly raining all day, again in Medellín. At the stoplight I was leaning my head on the side window because I was tired and feverish from a big cyst on my cheek. It was huge, ugly and throbbing. It seemed that the fever, the pain and the rain were forever. Again, I just felt lousy, and just wanted to get home, but the red light seemed to last forever. Then she tapped on my window. She was in her mid sixties, thin and smiling. In the light rain she was squinting as if it were bright sunlight. She was begging. I rolled down the window to give her a few coins, as she started her routine plea, but then she stopped when she saw my ugly cyst. She asked me if it hurt and told me to take the skin of a red tomato and place it on the sore all night. She touched my arm. She was my mother, my grandmother, my plate of cookies and milk in a warm kitchen. She was Margaret carrying me to the tub. The light changed and I drove ahead slower now. We forget how God packs love in the strangest places. At the stoplight, I could feel the warmth of love the way you can feel with your toes the warmth of the sun left in the sand on a cold night.

When I find her again, Kathy and I will take her to lunch. Maybe we will order her shrimp and chocolate. That will be a near perfect way to praise God. As John said in his gospel, the darkness will never understand nor overtake the light. Really, it is a miracle that there is any warmth at all in this universe. And one day, this warm love will be everywhere.

A few hours later, the doctor visited me in the recovery room to see how I was. I told him I needed to take a leak like a racehorse because I could not make myself urinate in the bedpan. He said, "Then get up and go to the bathroom." Afraid to move, much less try to get up, I said, "I can't" and he said, "You can." I said, "But I just had surgery" and he asked, "Who is telling you to get up?" and I said, "My doctor." And he said, "So, arise, walk and urinate." I was surprised I could get up and walk to the bathroom where I was sweetly delivered. We need to remember who it is who tells us, "Stop fearing. Only believe. Get over it." Faith is nothing private. We cannot eat without trusting the butcher and the baker, and we cannot see without trusting the candlestick maker. We cannot cross a street without trusting the red light to hold back tons of metal power. Who installed the cable in the elevator and who could have spit in the water?

Most of my trusting is as easy as breathing. I trust the air is good. I trust the bank to guard my money, but to trust this doctor? This weekend here in Medellín, Colombia, I will stand before thousands of people who trust me to give them a word, to feed their hearts with the word of God. They will hand me their hearts for a few minutes. They trust me to trust.

Feeling Lousy for Years

Not long after back surgery, I became worn down and sick. I had many exams but stumped the doctors. My bones ached and I felt like I had a fever all the time, especially after a busy weekend. The only doctor who could find something wrong with me was Dr. Stephen Duncan, a holistic doctor in Plano, Texas. He looked at my blood under a microscope and put me on a new diet. The day before my visit with him, I was having coffee with the one of the pastors of Gateway Church who was ministering freedom. I lifted my cappuccino high in the air and said, "The last thing I will be free from is coffee." I loved coffee. I even named our home groups, *Grupos de Café*. But now twelve hours later, the doctor looked over his glasses and asked me if I enjoyed my coffee yesterday. I said I sure did and he said, "Good, because that was your last one." I thought he was kidding, but it was my last cup. For some reason, my blood type, O-negative, cannot handle it. I changed my eating habits and began to take rest more seriously. Slowly like a ship turning around, my health returned.

But for many years I fought with it. Another pastor came over to my house and asked me how I could keep praying for the sick and see healings when I remained sick. He was compassionate but struggled with the question of wounded healers. I told him I didn't know but asked him to pray for me. One night I tried to research my symptoms on the Internet and was convinced I was going to die. I would start feeling better for a few days and then fall back into aching bones, chills in my back and fatigue. It is hard for anyone to endure sickness for a week or a month, but when it extends for years, we may stop believing healing will come. Back to waterskiing; we must hold on to the rope no matter how much water crushes us, and in time we are lifted up. I took comfort that Jesus healed a man who was sick for thirty-eight years (John 5:5), but on the other hand, Proverbs 13:12 haunted me:

> *Hope deferred makes the heart sick: but when*
> *the desire is fulfilled, it is a tree of life.*

(KJV 2000)

My hope was deferred and it was making my heart sick. Was this verse telling me that long-term disappointment sickens the heart—so deal with it? My good friend Dr. Crandall would ask over and over, "But Andrew, are you depressed?" and I'd tell him I was only depressed because I was still sick. One day I studied the Hebrew of the text and discovered the word *deferred* meant, *dragged*. I was dragging my hope behind me instead of having my hope out in front of me! The Bible tells us not to let a history of disappointment drag our life down. The future must have more influence than our past. Real hope is out in front, in the future. We must not let the weight of past disillusionments pull us back from hoping for a better future. Since the future is where I plan to live, I decided to focus on the future and to see myself strong and healed. And the ship began to turn around.

One of the hardest parts of dealing with sickness was Saturday evenings. Our first Saturday services started at 4 p.m. and I would start to feel miserable around 2 p.m. For three years, almost every Saturday afternoon around 3:00 p.m. the thunder would announce another hard rain. Around 3:30 p.m. the rain would fall, and I would drag myself to the lowest attended service of the weekend. It seemed the people were dragging. Very few healings happened. Not many new people came to the Lord, maybe five to eight people as compared to the other three services where up to fifty would come to Christ in each. I knew it was important if only one person came to Jesus, but I battled the oppression. Kathy was convinced witches were attending our services and pointed out a few to the intercessors. I would say a thousand witches do not have the right or the authority to oppress an anointed man. Nevertheless, I was plowing hard terrain.

One Saturday afternoon around 3 p.m., the rain clouds were forming in the west and I was praying in our closed-in porch. I was on my knees; our dog thought I wanted to play. Praying and playing can seem very similar. When I looked up, I saw it was lightly raining inside in a small space of about three square yards inside the house. I rubbed my eyes and looked again. For about thirty seconds I watched it rain. I did not feel anything, but I knew either my eyes were playing tricks on me or it was a spiritual rain. Suddenly, it stopped and the dog was still wagging her tail. I didn't think too much about it, but I mentioned it to my wife.

Two weeks later on Saturday afternoon again, it was about to rain. I walked outside to the backyard, and I could see it was lightly raining. Again, I didn't feel the rain. I focused my eyes and could see the rain falling all around me, but I noticed there was no rain wetting the street. I looked on the windows of the car parked in the road and there was no sign of rain, and yet it was raining. I called up to Kathy to come and see the rain. She came outside and squinted but saw nothing. I said, "Honey Bun, look. It is raining here and there." After a few minutes, she began to see the wet-less rain. For about twenty minutes we just looked and wondered what this meant. Was it just the power of suggestion? It was too clear for that. Surely, the Lord was saying He was about to pour out a greater rain. Suddenly it just stopped and we got ready for the evening service.

That night we shared about the rain we saw, but nobody seemed to be interested. I might as well have been talking about the price of potatoes in China. I tried to explain how God was preparing us for a fresh downpour of the Spirit. Again, Chinese potatoes. The following Saturday, Kathy left for church early while I stayed home to pray and battle against the darkness. The thunder boomed and black clouds formed in the sky at 3:30 p.m. right on cue. But this time, it rained and hailed. As I drove to church, the roads were flooded as never before and I almost did not make it. When I arrived, the lights were out and I heard a lady praying in a megaphone. The rain had knocked out the lights and flooded the sanctuary. The water broke through the roof, pouring right on the sound console. Just to make it interesting, a demonically oppressed man began to scream and punch the ushers. When they finally got him under control, Kathy called for a megaphone and led the church in warfare. Then she handed it over to one of the original members, Adriana, who let the devil have it. This sweet eighty-year-old lady was not going to let the devil mess with her church. I think she might have cussed at him. They were praying up a storm over the storm. As the prayer went ballistic, the ushers were sweeping out the water and others were holding down the crazy man. That is when I arrived and wondered what circus was in town, but I was happy to see the church excited and alive. Everyone was praying. I threw my notes away and someone brought two big torches. I began to preach in the torchlight. I felt like I was in the catacombs of Rome preaching to the first century church. Something was happening in the atmosphere. From then on, the 4:00 p.m. service changed. The freedom and the presence of God were more palpable and the attendance more than doubled. By the way, it hardly ever rains now at 3:30 p.m. If it does, it only is a light rain and it never affects the attendance or the joy. God likes to make streams in the desert and freedom in the hardest places.

The Dreams of Weakness into Strength

Dreams come like unexpected snow. You wake up from a dream and everything is covered with new meaning. In August 2014, the church in Medellín was growing in strength, and I was heading to speak in a stadium event in South Carolina, planning to rest in Florida for a few weeks with the family. I was riding a wave.

Two nights before the trip, I dreamed I was in a dimly lit church in Medellín. Rodney Howard Browne was in the front row preparing to preach when I greeted him. He said he heard about what God was doing in the city, and I said, "Rodney, I have learned the secret is that when we present our weakness to God, He presents His strength to us." We both sensed the cloud of the Spirit forming over us and I awoke refreshed. Since Rodney is known as a father of revival, I felt pleased with his approval in the presence of God.

The next night I dreamed again. I was trying to put a handmade canoe into a man-made canal that was more like a grey cement swimming pool. The canoe was heavy and very difficult to lower into the canal. I remember thinking that even if I could lower it into the water, it would not be worth it. I wanted blue flowing water. I pulled up the canoe and put it on top of my open convertible to drive away through a beautiful small town. On the way out of town, I saw my son, Christian, standing in front of a beautiful home. I asked him what he was doing there and he said it was Rodney's house. I stopped and knocked on the door. Rodney invited us inside his home overlooking the Intracoastal Waterway to dine with him and his wife, Adonica. Upon entering, I saw through the huge bay windows the bright crystal blue water of the Intracoastal. I turned to tell him about dream I had the night before, "Rodney, I told you I have learned the secret that when we present our extreme weakness, God presents His extreme power to us." I have never dreamed about a dream before. Suddenly, like in the first dream, the presence of the Holy Spirit settled over the four of us, and the beautiful water was flowing in the background.

I shared the dream with my wife and son, but thought no more about it. We flew to South Carolina where I expected to speak to 30,000 people in a baseball stadium. The organizers dreamed of transforming Myrtle Beach and expected the mayor and several city council members to be present. When we arrived, we drove up to a near empty parking lot. The city had canceled the permit to have the event in the stadium and now the stage was set up in the parking lot. Worse, only about fifty people showed up. I preached with all my heart about God's desire to transform people, families and cities. I preached about the power of expectation to the little flock of fifty. I spoke again the next day and there were even less people blinking in the sun drinking root beers. We were all feeling a little weak in our quest to transform a city, but that Sunday I preached in a wonderful church, the Father's House. I thought at least I could get back to a needed rest in Florida. But my sister, Mardi, called to tell me our mother's health was failing fast and I needed to be there. I rented a car and drove nine hours through heavy rain.

The next eight days, Mardi and I cared for our mom, whose kidneys were failing. She was almost ninety-four. We packed up her belongings and moved her to an assisted living home near my sister's home. I felt so weak praying for my Mom without seeing any results. I was exhausted and selfish. I wanted to leave and go fishing and at the same time, I wanted to stay and do everything I could to care for Mom. Her field hockey—ice-skating-tennis body was collapsing. She knew she was moving for the last time.

On the night before the move, she said, "You know, when you leave me, it probably will be the last time we see each other." I had to turn my head to look at the tennis on the television to hide my tears. Later I said, "Mom, we will always see each other again." But when I did drive away from the assisted living home, I cried all the way to the Interstate, as she had done when she dropped me off at boarding school. I had to head back to Colombia where I was a strong pastor leading the church into new territory. But on the Interstate, I was a little man crying behind the windshield wipers. I was glad it was raining so no one could see.

On the plane, I sensed the Lord telling me to read Matthew 14 and I said why? And he said, "Do you know what is in Matthew 14?" I didn't, so I read about John the Baptist being beheaded by Herod after a big birthday party. His disciples recovered the body but they could not recover the head. It was probably thrown out with the party trash. They must have felt pretty weak against a government that celebrated birthdays with decapitations.

Later on, the disciples were alone in a boat in a storm. In the dark, they could barely see Jesus walking on the waves. They screamed like schoolgirls because they thought he was a water demon. The future of the church was this group of twelve men screaming in the dark angry sea. After revealing Himself, Jesus calmed the sea but not their nerves.

What struck me was what happened between the execution and the storm—Jesus fed the multitude. Jesus heard the tough news about John and tried to hide in a desolate place, but the people found Him. People of all ages, old and young, sick and tormented. And they were hungry. And it was here between the cruelty of man and the cruelty of storms that Jesus did something so beautiful. He fed them all and no one was left out. No one was looking at his neighbor's lunch with envy. For that hour, everyone was content. The power of God was like the unseen undertow that pulled everyone into a place of peace. The people never forgot it and we have never forgot. This miracle only happened because Jesus felt weak at the news of John. He needed to be alone in his weakness in a lonely place. And there in the desolate place, the people came needing a miracle, and it was there that Jesus looked into the heavens and broke the bread that kept on breaking and breaking.

Then it hit me. If I let my heart keep on breaking for the old, for my mother, for the children on the street, for my childhood friends growing grey and for the lonely, then I will see the quiet power of God. Perhaps His greatest miracle happened because He had to withdraw to a lonely place. His cousin was murdered and He knew His own murder would be worse. Maybe in the midst of the success of the multitudes, He almost forgot this world was so cruel. Maybe He was tempted to think He could continue His ministry for many years and enjoy the festivals with His family, dying in peace at an old age like Abraham. That wouldn't be bad. But now the death of John the Baptist was ice water on His face, and Jesus wanted to curl up alone with the Father. And there in the weakness, the compassion exploded in His heart and He said, "Bring the fish and the bread to Me." The people sat down everywhere. He looked into the heavens. No one spoke—only the voice of Jesus blessing the bread by the sea, which was beginning to churn. The voice of Jesus, washed clean from crying a few hours earlier, was now blessing thousands.

I arrived in Colombia for the healing conference with Randy Clark. As soon as I landed, my sister again called me to say the end was coming sooner than we thought. I had to wait a day to find a flight back. I was a mess. I broke just trying to receive an offering for the conference. I had to fly all day, rent a car and drive over the mountains to try to get there before Mom died. I arrived on the next day before noon. Mom only recognized me and smiled. She tried to speak but there was no force to push out the words. Smiling and looking at each other would have to do.

My sister, who had taken such good care of Mom for so long, needed to go home to rest. Since the nurses thought she would hang on for a few more days, my sister urged me to stay the night at her house, but after dinner, I returned to be alone with Mom for the next four hours. I just knew I had to be there. I called Kathy and, over the phone, we prayed and worshipped. When I hung up, I told Mom, who was sleeping, I would be there with her all night. I turned to make up the sofa bed, turned again and she was gone. I thanked God for her life. I held her hand so thin and white, yet beautiful. As I knelt crying, I noticed the pain was not cruel. It was painful but not horrible. It was peaceful pain. It was my heart coming alive, remembering love.

When I stood in the old Episcopal Church in White Solapur Springs to give her eulogy, my heart was like a child trying to not spill a hot cup of coffee as he brought it to his father. I was burning inside, trying to hold back the tears. Mardi was, too, but we made it. Then alone we let the hot cups spill everywhere. In our weakness, our relationship is stronger. In weakness, I returned to Colombia to preach and they looked into my eyes to see if I was more alive. And I, trembling, brought them a little cup of life. I told them about Mom with a broken heart like bread.

Almost Kicked the Bucket

A year later, I was having arterial spasms but the stress tests were not revealing anything. Then Dr. Parga took a long look at the test and said, "A positive negative." What? He was saying what looks good isn't.

The spasms were getting stronger and they rushed me to hospital where they put in two stents. I was awake but drugged enough to ask the doctors and nurses in the surgery room, "Do you know how to keep an idiot in suspense? I will tell you after the procedure." They still did a good job but for the next ten days the spasms continued until I passed out in the house in front of Kathy and Andrew Michael. My first ride in an ambulance was no fun. Once in the hospital, they couldn't find a pulse. I almost left earth then. They kept me there for three days without a clue as to what was wrong. Kathy had half the city praying. Churches from all around were praying. I would cry every time I heard of another pastor praying. I think we are more connected than we think. During that time, a great missionary to Colombia, Bob Finke, was struck and killed in Bogota by a motorcycle. People said they felt the enemy darkening the skies. But Kathy refused to let me go. The head nurse told her she had to leave the intensive care unit but Kathy made her back off. I remember looking over one night seeing her get a few minutes of sleep in the chair next to my bed and wondered where that kind of love comes from.

The spasms continued but all the doctors were leaving for the three-day weekend. One doctor turned around and looked at my latest halter results, and with the recommendation of Dr. Chauncey Crandall, took me for another catheterization to save my life again. After a week in the hospital, the spasms stopped but I was as weak as a starfish on the beach. It took two more months to recover because my thyroid was out of whack.

During this time, the pastoral team rose together to a new level. The church kept growing. The bonds between us deepened. And the prayer life of the church reached higher. I was so weak. During the recovery, I was deeply depressed. Once when alone in the house, I told God all this confessing the Word does not work because I was not getting better. Kathy would come back and ask me what I was confessing. I wanted to tell her I was confessing the part where Paul said women should be quiet. But I kept confessing and suddenly, with the help of some good doctors in the States, healing happened. Paul said he boasted of his weakness, not in spite of, so that the glory of Christ would be revealed. I was living in the "so that." In my weakness, my home, my church and my city seemed to get stronger, which I had tried to do for so long in my own strength.

TWENTY ONE

Miscellaneous Miracles

Often we limit miracles to divine healings, supernatural protection or last minute provisions, but God has a lot of ways to crack reality. There are signs and wonders, and then some signs that just make us wonder.

Stock Market and Termites

When we rented an old house in Cali, Colombia, it gnawed on me that termites were tunneling through the beams in my office ceiling. I worried about that. Everyday the termite droppings on the floor bored into my peace. I wondered how I could kill the termites. Suddenly one day, the owner told us we had to leave because he had sold the house to a man who was going to demolish the house and build apartments. Six months later, I stood in front of the empty lot where the house was. I looked up to where my office was and remembered how I would worry about the termites in the beams. And now the beams don't exist and the termites are gone.

We had our retirement savings in the stock market and the little dips would gnaw at me. When I had to minister to our church plants in the mountains, I was out of touch with the stock markets, and I arrived home to see the red numbers, sometimes one to two percent of their value. Then 9-11 hit and we lost more than seventy percent of our value. Many of the stocks went belly up and never recovered. It was like looking at where the house once was. I used to agonize over seeing the market fall hour by hour, but the huge drop was almost refreshing. Shock is better than slow agony. Big changes don't seem to worry us as much as the little ones

In England before World War II, about fifteen percent of the population dealt with extreme depression and worry, which gnawed on them like termites. When the war broke out, depression almost disappeared. Everyone was suffering together with joy. Then at the end of the war, the depression surged back to fifteen percent. It seems we need to have peaceful conditions to be able to worry.

On the night of October 27, 2008, I dreamed the DOW shot up 900 points. In the dream I was watching the television and the DOW surged to 900; then I woke up. I shared the dream with my wife, my boys and Pastor Randy. I didn't think too much about it the next morning, but I did notice the market was up 500 points at noon. So, during the last hour of the market, I was on the phone with Randy and rooting for the DOW to hit 900. It did. That was October 28, 2008. I didn't make any money on the tip, but I think God gave me the tip to show me that He knows how to tip anything toward us. Letting money problems gnaw at us is not a money problem but a heart problem, a trust problem. He is the owner of the house. He lets us live here. He will take care of the beams. If He takes away the house, we will have another.

I am ashamed to admit I let money gnaw at me for years. It is a missionary work hazard. We had invested a great deal of our savings into the church plant in Medellín, and for the first twenty years on the field, we did not receive a salary from Colombia. We lived on our savings and the donations from some amazing friends and churches in the States. Ten years ago, we started to receive a modest salary from the church in Medellín but we still had to sell our getaway apartment in Florida. I was constantly trying to calculate how could we buy another home. College, health and the unexpected were eating away our savings. I finally made a decision before the Lord to praise Him for taking care of me now and forever. If we are not worried about who will pay the light bills for eternity, we can trust him for this sliver of time called life. I learned that prosperity does not bring peace but peace brings prosperity. And peace brings the great capacity to enjoy what we have.

Holy Mackerel

When I fish, I don't relax. I work three or more rods—bottom fishing, casting lures, throwing a cast net, fishing with live bait and using a sabiki rig to catch more live bait. I run up and down the beach, looking for any sign of fish, casting, baiting and changing lures. And many times I have said like Peter, "Lord, I fished all night and caught nothing." I would add, "and I fished really hard."

On August 30, 2011, Kathy and I were resting for a week in Florida to celebrate our twenty-five years of marriage. We went down to the beach to vacate our home while a realtor showed it to a potential buyer. For years I had been working hard to supplement our income to hold on to our home. On top of ministry, I ran up and down Colombia to promote several businesses. I caught nothing. So I was resigned to selling our home, but I was still fishing hard.

As Kathy sat in the beach chair, I worked four rods. From 5 p.m. till 8 p.m., I caught nothing. I was resigned to pack up the rods and head home. Kathy came down by my side. My lines were reeled in and I was holding on to a pole with the lure dangling from the top. It was a small flag of surrender. In the salmon-colored horizon, we turned to walk toward the gear. Suddenly, like a flashing spear, a Spanish mackerel jumped out of the blue sea onto the beach. It landed right at our feet inches away. In all my fishing years, I never had seen anything like it. I have seen small baitfish jump on the beach, but never a meal-sized fish. Kathy yelled, "Grab it. Grab it." I tried to grab it but the mackerel was slick and almost electric. Finally, I was able to grasp it and throw it up higher on the beach. After a few seconds, the mackerel lay still. Like someone trying to learn a new language, the mouth slowly opened and closed. There was no coin in its mouth but its quiet words were some sort of currency. Kathy kept saying it was a sign and I kept saying that it was unbelievable. We both had to keep looking at it to believe it. I tossed it in the bucket, but it was hard for me to stop fishing. It always is. So, I threw in my lure a few more times, but then I noticed the fish was flapping itself down toward the water. If I didn't quit, I might lose the holy mackerel. It was time to rest. We headed home and I cleaned it. Kathy cooked it. We prayed and ate it. I almost had to chew the fish to believe it was real.

When Kathy and I were rookies on the mission field, we had a sign reading, "*Watch God Work*," and put it on our bathroom mirror. We so often try to help God work or plead for God to work, but just watching God work was different. And there on the Florida shore, we watched God throw a fish at us. Fishing has been the love language of my heart. God spoke to David with sheep. He spoke to farmers about seeds, to women about leaven and to Peter with fish. Two thousand years later, He told a fish to swim full blast toward us and jump. Of course, there could have been a shark chasing it and it was just a coincidence that we were standing in the very spot the mackerel would land, but that is a leap of faith too big for me. God was speaking a bright word to my heart.

Years ago when I first talked to Pastor Randy MacMillan, he told me the fish were jumping in the boat in Colombia. Only once in thirty years did I give an invitation to receive Jesus and no one came. Today we see well over a hundred swim to Jesus on a weekend, I suspect from this day it will be even greater.

We say, "Lord, we have fished all night, but nevertheless, at your word, we will cast the net." When we have tried every lure in the box, there is a swirl. Fish suddenly turn direction without any apparent reason. A thousand fish are coming our way.

As I write these lines, I am looking over a small lake outside of our new home in Florida. My mother left an unexpected inheritance, which was just enough to buy the apartment. We named the lake, *Lake Charlotte.*

Carried to the Table

I was whacking through my emails when I saw a request from Lynette Brenner of New Jersey to pray for her friend, Ruth Yost. She was dying and the doctors had notified the family. I was exhausted emotionally and physically. I just wanted to get out of town to rest, read and fish. I prayed about a 2.4 second prayer, short even for a bull ride. Basically I punted with no hang time. I mumbled, "Heal 'er Jesu…" and was about to delete it, but my finger froze over the delete button. I never had met Ruth Yost nor did I have room on my emotional plate for another burden. I wanted to get out of town. As a pastor, I wanted to plead with my church, "Please, just behave and don't do anything stupid for one week. Please." So, Lynette hits me with this request from a thousand miles away, but suddenly the importance of one life tugged on my cranky, tired heart. I stopped and prayed and waited to see if a word would float to the surface of my conscience.

Ruth was bleeding internally and the doctors were not able to stabilize her blood platelets. She was 1,000 and normal is 200,000. I was thinking it was time to pray for her family to be comforted. Maybe it was time to delete her. About 300,000 people die everyday on this planet. Life goes on. Death happens 300,000 times a day! One hundred percent of the people in Africa die eventually. Remarkably, the United States has the same statistics. And Colombia. And New Jersey. So let's pray something sweet and move on. In the midst of so much suffering, what is the life of one lady?

Somehow this lady got my attention. Ruth was like the sick lady in the Bible who heard that Jesus was passing by. He was on an important mission with his important men, all filled with a sense of importance. Thousands of people crowded around and each one had important issues. In the swirl of all this importance, she sticks out her boney finger and touches Jesus. He slams on the breaks and wants to know who had touched Him with that tug of faith. She stopped the whole parade just for her little healing. Have you ever had one person in a crowd get your attention?

As I waited, I believe Jesus spoke to me. Really. Have you ever been so tired that you are looking at words on a page but your eyes are not focused on the words, much less on the meaning of the words. Then suddenly, you focus and realize you are looking at words that say something? I was waiting to receive direction from God and I suddenly realized that His words were already there in my mind, waiting for me to see them. This came to mind: "Like King David carried Mephibosheth to the table, tell Ruth I am carrying her to My table of healing."

There is the beautiful story of King Saul's crippled son, Mephibosheth who thought the new king, David, was out to kill him, but David was out to kill him with kindness. Mephibosheth saw himself as a dog and when David's soldiers knocked on his door, he thought he was a dead dog. The soldiers surprised him and carried him to the king's table where he ate like a king. Sometimes we are so weak we can't even crawl to His table; somebody carries us. Sometimes we are so hurt, we can't even imagine that there is such a table, and somebody carries us.

So I wrote Lynette to tell Ruth that Jesus was carrying her to the table. She did, and a week later, Jesus carried her. I received this email from Ruth:

Dear Andrew,
You prayed for me, at Lynette Brenner's request, and received a message of healing for me. Last week they were notifying my next of kin and three days later I was home and healed, inside and out. To say thank you is so puny compared to the

gratitude I have for you and for our God. God bless you in your work. You are the hands and feet of our Lord.

With deepest gratitude,

Ruth Yost

She thinks I had something to do with it! I was about to delete her. Her faith stopped Jesus and, I believe, Jesus stopped my finger above the delete button. That's how it works. We can't pray for the 300,000 about to die today, but we can pray for that pesky person who tugs on Jesus, who tugs on us. Look around. Do you think you got here on your own? At some point, somebody carried you, too.

I think one of the reasons we have seen many signs, miracles and wonders is because we have an atmosphere of faith energized by love (Galatians 5:6). The miracles do not spin around anyone's ministry gift. I am not God's man of power for the hour because most of the miracles flow through the hands of the people. Often when people give their testimony of being healed from cancer or cardiac problems, I secretly hope they say, "When Pastor Andres prayed for me..." but almost always they mention some home group leader or just a friend.

Resurrection by a Lukewarm Christian

Jota was slipping away from the church, attending the university and driving a special cab that picked up drunks in bars outside of the city. On the way to pick up a client, Jota saw a man who'd been thrown about thirty feet from his motorcycle and was lying in a hole. When he approached the man, he saw that his torso and neck were completely distorted—half of the man's body faced upright and the bottom half upside down. His head was stuck against his shoulder at an unnatural angle, and Jota could see it was clearly broken. The color of his skin, his lifeless eyes, and the lack of a pulse assured Jota that he was dead.

His companion told him to leave the dead man alone but Jota sensed the love of Jesus compelling him to pray. He prayed and the man opened his eyes, took a deep breath and began to move. He began to untwist and his head turned around straight. When Jota tells it, he cries and says the real resurrection was inside his own heart. When the medics arrived and saw the the state of the motorcycle, they could not believe the man was still alive with all his bones intact. Jota and his friend were now at least thirty minutes behind schedule, but suddenly, he found himself at the bar on time. To this day, he cannot explain what happened. It's amazing how God will use anyone who is willing to say yes!

In our church, the *one to another* ministry is activated and cultivated. In the New Testament, we find sixty *"one to another"* exhortations—pray for one another, exhort one another, etc. I think this is God's Plan A, or it just may be my excuse for not personally moving more in the gifts. My heart is to see every member a minister, moving in the gifts of the Holy Spirit. For example, one day my son Christian was at the altar at the end of a service, questioning if God ever wanted to use him for miracles. Suddenly from the platform, I said, "Christian, come here. God wants to use you." I called him to my side and said I felt God wanted to heal women with serious problems in their abdominal area. Three women came forward. When Christian gently prayed for them, each one felt something so dramatic, they cried with joy. Each one said the pain had disappeared. Another time, Christian prayed for a man who was just released from jail for murder. They released him because his heart was failing. He was number 10,000 on the heart transplant list. Christian prayed and told him God was going to do something amazing. The very next day, they called him in for the heart transplant. Guillermo thinks it was a *clerical error*, but he knows God used Christian.

Machetes & Knives

One sermon I thought I was preaching about life and death issues but obviously failing because when a man came into the building screaming and waving a machete in one hand and a knife in the other, everyone forgot about my great sermon and looked his way. I saw everyone stand up and look to my right but I had no idea what was happening. I could feel the wave of fear. Finally, I focused on the young man against the wall flashing the machete. Since I had the microphone and was the pastor, I had to act pastor-like and tell everyone to just pray quietly as I walked toward the crazy man. I had no idea what I was going to do.

Years before, I was praying for people after a service in a town of Yumbo, Colombia. Some young men told me they had a demon-possessed girl upstairs in the church office. So like a big shot I said, "Take me to her." Somehow I did not hear them mention that she had a knife. When I walked in the office and two guys were trying to hold her. I told them to let her go. They asked me if I was sure and I was, until I saw the knife, but they had already released her. Too proud to tell them to grab her again, I tried calmly to order her to drop the knife, which she did after five minutes. Then Jesus washed her in His love and she cried for a long time. It ended well, barely.

So now years later, what was I going to do? As I approached the young man, a big guy, Rodrigo, tackled him from behind and all the ushers pounced on him. No one was hurt and they dragged the poor fellow out, kicking and screaming. What was interesting is that Rodrigo told his friend earlier that morning he had had a dream where the devil was going to attack the church. Rodrigo came prepared.

A month later an usher tells me that the same guy wants to apologize to me. I said sure, but I wanted company. When I saw the young timid man, I thought he did not seem dangerous. When he asked me for forgiveness, I said yes but looked to see if his hands were empty before hugging him. Later he told an usher why he did it. He said the devil told him in a dream to kill Pastor Andrew. When he asked why, the devil said, "Because he tells jokes." I have never been so encouraged to keep telling jokes in my preaching. Poor devil.

TWENTY TWO

Contagious Love

Besides my salvation and my family, the greatest gift God has given me is this supernatural love for the people of Medellín. The church was born in my heart. While still living in Cali, I would pray for Medellín. I had not yet seen Medellín but when I prayed for her, I felt a white-hot love erupting from the Spirit. I know I am a selfish person who often prays selfishly for my life and my family, "Bless us four and no more," but Jesus gave me the gift of loving a people I had never seen. Once I saw them, I loved them more. How did Jesus fit a big city in my little, selfish heart?

One of the greater honors in my life was being presented the "Son of Antioquia" award, which the State Assembly awarded to me for the church's work with the children and the poor. I usually don't like award ceremonies, but I ate this one up. With a military band, medals, ribbons, certificate and long speeches, I was like a kid grinning shamelessly from ear to ear. Then I got to preach Jesus in the assembly chamber.

I like going to our church now, but in the early days it was horrible. Every service was a battle and the atmosphere seemed so heavy it was hard to breathe. During worship the people mouthed the songs like fish trying to breathe out of water. When I preached, they looked at me as Randy would say, with their heads tilted like *papagayos*. It seemed every Sunday we had to dig a new well to get a little bit of water.

Now we just show up and the river is flowing. And thank God the river does not depend on me.

One lady, Olga, had half of her lung removed and she was breathing with difficulty. Her home group prayed for her, and the following week her X rays revealed her lung had completely grown back. Go figure. Another home group testified of a baby who was born dead. The nurses were going to take the little body to the morgue, but the group of women demanded they leave the baby in the room for a while. They prayed heaven down until the baby started to cry. The baby is now a young boy doing fine. It seems almost every week there is a report of cancer or tumors disappearing. Last year in the Fresh Wind Foundation, a two-year old boy, Manuel, was malnourished and developing poorly. He was listless with little movement or expression. One day he quit breathing and turned purple. The workers in the foundation did not have time to call Tom, the director, or me, but they did call upon the Lord and laid hands on the boy. After forty minutes, he came alive. They went wild. But the best part is that Manuel is now responding, talking and walking. It seems the break from life served him well.

Some of the wildest miracles happen in our weekend retreats for new believers. We have a farm where we will have between forty to a hundred new believers spend two nights with a group of leaders every weekend. They receive a crash course on the Cross, repentance and faith. Most are filled with the Holy Spirit and are baptized in water. Just last year as a group of leaders were ministering to a man, who was a warlock. He fell to the floor, groaning and spewing at the mouth. As the leaders were trying to cast out the demons, dozens of buzzards landed on top of the building. This has never happened before. They kept praying until one leader with great authority commanded the demons to leave. At the same time the man was set free, the buzzards suddenly flew away. I don't understand it all, but there is a lot more going on in the spiritual dimension than we think.

But God uses the pastors, too. Pastor Juan David, just sent me an email about a crusade he had in a small town. About five hundred people were gathered in the town's plaza when an elderly man fell down. They saw that he was not breathing and had no pulse. Juan and his wife, Marili, prayed for about thirty minutes, but the man's body grew colder and more rigid. When they rebuked the spirit of death and called on the spirit of life in Jesus Christ to come, the man took a deep breath and opened his eyes. Within minutes he was walking around the plaza as the people shouted, "He's alive! He's alive!" Juan said that jump-started the crusade.

Not all miracles have been so easy for them. Their grandson, Andrés Felipe, contracted salmonella at six months of age. For the next six months Andrés suffered convulsions and hemorrhages, nearly dying several times. Three times they had to revive him. The doctors said if he lived, he would never walk or talk. With the entire church praying, the boy recovered and now is talking, playing soccer, and preaching, if you give him a microphone.

Pastors Lucho and Luz Victoria Padilla see miracles in marriages every week. When I hear of some of the problems of a married couple, I think they need a referee or a lawyer, but Lucho and Luz V believe in total restoration. When they have their romance nights in the church with a thousand couples, there is a constant stream of testimonies of how Jesus caused them to fall in love again. I can throw Lucho the biggest angriest bear, the worst marriage, and he knows how to tame it. They have a file full of testimonies of men who fell in adultery, but the faith and forgiveness of their wives pulled them out. Many of these couples now lead home groups for couples. Lucho just emailed me the story of Jazmine, who had stomach and thyroid cancer. After excruciating treatment, she survived, but the doctors told her she would be barren. She said I prayed for her and said her name would be Life and that she would have a child. I don't remember any of this but she now has a beautiful, six-month-old girl in her arms.

Pastors Adolfo and Lucelida Cuellar are always giving me the latest miracle report. I never get tired of the story of Dr. Issac Gaviria, the director of a trade school, who was in the hospital for a lung transplant. Adolfo went right to Dr. Gaviria's wife in the waiting room and declared in a loud voice, "Life. Life in Jesus' name," while stretching his hand toward the surgery room. People thought he was crazy, but right at that moment Dr. Gaviria saw angels fill the room. As he tells it, he did not have a vision or a dream of angels; he clearly saw hundreds of angels crammed inside the operating room during the surgery, as he was floating away from his body. The operation was a success. He is the only survivor of twelve lung transplants in that hospital. When I visited him in his home a month later, he told me he had a problem. He starts to pray around 9 p.m. and feels the love of God so thick around himself that he cannot stop praying until around 3 a.m. His face was beaming as he told me this. I told him I hoped to have the same problem.

God has given us amazing youth pastors. Jerry and Barbara Manderfield got the youth group going, then their son, Joel, with his bride, Gisi, took it to a new level. Now, an ex-soccer player, Juan Guillermo Ricuarte, and his wife, Liliana, have taken the youth to new heights. Juan was a nationally-known soccer player, but came to our church and was willing to work as a janitor. He was a good soccer player. He was a good janitor, too but now he is an excellent pastor. He has 1,800 youth passionately worshiping God. Recently, Juan teamed up with another famous soccer star to found an outreach in the most dangerous neighborhood in Medellín, La Sierra. Even the police are afraid to go there. More than a hundred youth from the Sierra now serve the church. More than a thousand will gather around the soccer field to listen to Juan talk about the blood of Jesus washing away the blood of guilt. These guys are nation shakers.

Our children's pastors, Rafael and Paola, were young and preparing for professional careers, until an encounter with the Holy Spirit. During a conference in our church, they experienced the power of

God electrocuting them so much that they both trembled for days. They began dating soon thereafter, got married and were ordained as pastors of the children's church. Rafi and Paola have never believed the Holy Spirit in the kids was a little one, but the same big Holy Spirit who raised Jesus from the dead. They taught the kids how to worship, heal the sick and win the lost. During our annual pastor's conference with up to a thousand pastors, the kids come to lay hands on the sick and hurting pastors; the tears flow. Rafa and Paola have also trained and imparted the vision for the children's church to more than a thousand churches with their own conferences. Rafa once gave me two candles, one burned down and short and the other tall. He said the tall candle represents the kids. The short candles represent the adults because they have burned away most of their life. Now where should we invest our focus? Maybe that is why we invest so much into our children's foundation.

Pastors Tom and Jennifer have raised the children's foundation to new heights prioritizing love and the presence of the Holy Spirit. All the staff—the nutritionists, the psychologists and the workers—stay in the flow of the love of the Spirit. At this time, we have about two hundred kids who live in nearby homes of single moms lost in drugs and prostitution.

I love telling the story about one of the kids, a four-year old boy named Stiven, who fell four stories headfirst on hard concrete. The doctors didn't think he'd live. At best, they said he would be a vegetable. Staff members went with Stiven's mom to the Intensive Care Unit to pray for him, and suddenly, Stiven began to move his extremities. Days later he was sitting up and talking. Months later, he was back to running around full speed in the Foundation. Another favorite is about the fifteen-month-old toddler whose mom brought him to the Foundation, but she viscerally hated anything to do with God. Many women tried to share Christ with her, but she would get angry with them. One day her son was playing with a toy when his dad put a worship CD that a staff worker had given to him. The toddler began to raise his hands and close his eyes, twirling in circles and smiling. When the mom saw this, she fell to her knees to accept Jesus. She said, "I could no longer resist God when I she saw my baby feeling so happy in the presence of God."

I left out the stories of most of the pastors and I left out ninety-nine percent of the miracles in the church. I could tell you about Orlando, who was diagnosed with leukemia. People prayed. Though I was surprised by the doctors' report declaring him healed, Orlando wasn't. "Pastor, we prayed didn't we? Well. Here is answer."

The atmosphere of the Spirit hovering over the church makes it easier to believe, but why do miracles seem to happen more here than in the States? The simple reason is when people talk about God doing *God-things*, God does things. The word, testimony, means in the Hebrew "to do it again." When an ordinary person tells of an extraordinary miracle of God, it creates the atmosphere for it to happen again. If someone shares about being healed from Crohn's Disease, a person with the same disease gets an instant download of faith for his or her healing. Where there is no testimony, faith doesn't happen, and nothing happens out of the ordinary. The Bible is so powerful because it is full of testimonies and they are for us. For years before my conversion, I would read the Bible to pull out deep thoughts, rich poetry or insights that I could toss into the mixture of religions that I called my beliefs. I read the Bible, but kept my respectable distance. It was an intellectual pursuit. The Bible was next to my poetry books of Rilke, Japanese haikus and William James' analytical books on the subjective religious experience. If I was caught reading the Bible, I could always pull out the other books and say, "See, I am not an idiot." But alone, reading the Bible was like working on the electrical wiring of an old house. I thought the electrical current was turned off, but it wasn't. That lady was smart to wrap her Bible in electrical tape.

Even after I became a Christian, I was not convinced of the historic validity of the Scriptures, but as I had more experiences with the supernatural, the "over and above natural" God of the Bible, I became convinced of its accuracy and of its high voltage. Much of the higher criticism of the Bible was birthed in the German Lutheran church, where for years no one had any kind of God encounter. So if you belong to a church where God never seems to intervene, it will affect your metaphysical presumption. You will assume you live in a closed, cause-and-effect universe, and so you will study the Bible with the presumption that miracles do not happen, prophecies do not really come to pass, and all the testimonies are mere human subjective meanderings. But when you study the Bible with the base presumption that God is alive and capable of popping through the cause-and-effect universe anytime He chooses, then your theology will change. You believe God creates everything from nothing, suspends the Red Sea, throws the fire of divine life into a virgin's womb and raises the cold dead man from the grave. It is all a matter of where you put the first brick of belief. You can put it in the closed universe worldview or you can start in the open "oh-my-God-He-is-alive" universe. It is not a matter of intelligence but will. Jesus said, "If anyone wants to do the will of My Father, he shall know of the doctrine, whether it be of God, or whether I am making it up" (John 7:17, author's paraphrase). What you believe is more a matter of your heart than your head. We think our head is so smart but it follows the heart like an obedient dog.

Where there are testimonies, faith happens, and faith makes things happen. So, hearing testimonies makes faith happen. Faith brings God on the scene. That's my theory and I'm sticking to it. And that is why I wrote this book: to bring testimonies like Jesus helping hang up a birdcage, like how a little bit of blue sky in a man's glasses could cause hope to flare up in my heart, and like how a simple conversation or book can change a destiny.

Epilogue

My professor at Yale, Henri Nouwen, said he pushed himself to write everyday. He would start writing anything and usually without feeling. He would push the pen over the paper, and suddenly, the lines would become alive. So, today I am writing these last lines hoping they will be like dazed fish that when released in the water, awake, shake and dart into the deep. Writing should be something alive in me darting into you.

After a long trip, I put my suitcases down to greet my family; I pick them up again, to carry them into my room and I am surprised they are so heavy. So it is when men retire: they take off the weight of deadlines, stress and decisions and are surprised how heavy the weight of the work was. But then they feel a heavier weight, as feels the phantom weight of an amputated leg. The pressure of a tight schedule turns into the dread of a short life. And the uneasiness of not getting things done turns into questioning if we have done anything at all. Suddenly it dawns on them that the heaviness of work was shielding them from the weightier matters of what really matters.

Along the beach, the retired walk furiously, trying to extend life a few years. Even at 55, we called ourselves as middle aged, as if we would live to a 110.

When we were kids and heard about an older person dying, we thought, "Oh well, he was old." But now that we are older, we think, "Oh, nuts." We pick up novels, hobbies, and new interests to buffer ourselves from thoughts like, "Where will I be five seconds after I die?" Maybe we are not afraid of death, but as Woody Allen said, we just don't want to be there when it happens. But we will be.

When the time comes, there will be someone there. This is the good news of the book of Hebrews telling us Jesus has come to deliver us from the life long fear of death. I like the bluntness of Paul declaring if the resurrection of Jesus was a hoax, we are really screwed (1 Corinthians 15:18-19). But he *is* alive and wants to clothe us with his goodness. Imagine looking forward to dying.

I dare you to imagine waking up in heaven. It would be like waking up as a kid again on the first day of an unending summer with everything bathed with gold. Trees would be even more like trees than they are on earth. There would be new colors and smells that you somehow knew existed. You could sleep in forgiveness. You could say what you mean to your family and friends. You could be peaceful enough to do a few things that really matter. The best part of heaven is that everything is out in the open and it's great.

The word *retirement* is not even in the Bible, but there is a time to step back and let more capable young men and women take on the heavier tasks. And in Christ, as we age, we can lean forward like hand gliders, confident the invisible will lift us higher.

Everything goes back in the box at the end of the game. Time takes away everything, but leaves more. Time seems like a thief but really is a secret giver. We get old, parents die, the children leave home and we lose touch with hundreds of friends. But strangely, the little conversations between a couple, the insignificant memories, and the hectic routines of the children, all begin to create over time a huge sense of home. Little things accumulate silently like snow at night, and suddenly you realize a family emerges. Time takes away almost everything, like waves clawing the sand from the beach, but time gives, too, like the waves leaving a cove or a coral ridge. Time leaves a deep understanding between couples and a deep sense of community among friends. Time seems like a thief, but really it is a secret giver. It gives us greater things like a thankful heart and a sense of home even in distant lands.

Time has taken the kids flying in and out of the house. Time took our youth and lots of options. It seems clear now that I will never be the coach of the Cleveland Browns. I will never ride a bull, even though I never wanted to. I've discovered my limits over the years. But time has left Kathy and me with a deep sense of peace. From all the residue of indistinguishable days, we have a shared history. A friend once said, "Look at my face. Time has not been kind to me." But time is kind. Left are the well-worn paths of communication of understanding—how to talk to each other and how we talk and listen to God.

All through the years, the one constant, Jesus, is there. He is not silent. To rephrase Simon & Garfunkel in "Sounds of Silence": "Hello God, my old friend. I've come to be with you again." Silence is wonderful, but God and silence together are better. Time reveals how huge our relationship with God is. Sand dunes are formed when an obstacle, a fence or a post, blocks the wind from carrying the sand away. That obstacle stays fixed in place and the sand builds around it. Sometimes we see God better when everything has been carried away except what is timeless and immovable. We see what God has held in place. As we take time to reflect on our life, we may notice some dunes where God has been standing quietly by our side.

Blue Mountains

When we celebrated our twenty-five years of marriage, Kathy and I bought a 2004 Chevy with a cassette player. I loved it because I have hundreds of cassettes with old music. Ten years ago I went to Singapore and walked around with a Walkman. The youth never had seen a cassette player and looked at me as if I just walked out of Dickens' *The Tale of Two Cities*. The cassettes don't have their full sound any more. Much of the music has evaporated over the years, but my memory fills the gaps. What I hear with my ears and what I hear with my memory merge into a deeper sound. Scientists have proven that our mind will unconsciously fill in missing letters, breaks in lines or lost images. The lack of fidelity of the tapes creates ditches where the warm water of memory fills and soaks the music.

Thirty years ago, Kathy and I stepped out of the church in New Jersey and onto the mission field. We have been faithful by grace to our vow, but we know we have not been faithful to that image of a perfect couple walking out of the church. We have suffered, stressed out and somehow sailed together into calm seas. Our bodies are not high fidelity, either. There are gaps. If our wedding picture is the song, we are the sound of an old tape. But we fill in the gaps and the music resonates deeper.

Sometimes the only way we really hear is by remembering. When Jesus told his disciples He was going to rise from the dead, it didn't sink in. After He rose from the dead, they remembered His words and it was like rain sinking into soft soil. Thousands of seeds uncurled into life. Many things Jesus said before now made sense in the new light. Often we remember something our parents said years later. When we first heard the words, we rolled our eyes; now remembering them, tears well in our eyes.

As a boy I remember thinking that the mountains in West Virginia looked like the blankets on my parents' bed. The distance softened the mountains with blue and plum purple. I knew that up close the mountains were rugged, broken with fallen trees and thatched with briers, but from afar, they seemed benevolent and soft, like blankets. Even raging stars are sweet when seen light years away. I used to think being close to the mountains told the hard truth about mountains, but now I think the distance reveals the mountains as they really are—benevolent.

As I said earlier, at the moment I proposed to Kathy, we sensed we were stepping into a destiny greater than us. It was like being on a huge ship that begins to move from the dock. The ship was so big you hardly noticed the movement, but it was now sailing. We did not understand all that God was going to do; the thousands of people, the churches, the miracles, the leaders. We did not know the amazing sons we would raise. We did not see the sleepless nights, the battles, the betrayals and the skirmishes with fear. We did not see the bullrings filled, the youth on fire, the miracles and the church plants. We did not see our times of exhaustion, brokenness and loneliness. We only saw the mountains, blue and sweet. Somehow we were remembering forward. And now we are looking at the coming years of marriage and ministry, and we see the blue mountains where we will die. It is a beautiful thing.

I saw the blue in the skies of childhood. I saw the blue in the glasses of the man looking at the sky with his arms crossed on the campus of the University of Virginia. I saw the blue in my dreams of flowing waterways and blue trees. I saw the blue in the eyes of people, like Heidi Baker and Dr. Crandall, carrying heaven. This morning I see the blue of the sea and am quite certain that one day in heaven I will see a blue I have never seen, but always knew was there.

I called the church in Charlottesville where the man with blue in his glasses was looking at the sky. They gave me the name and number of the pastor who was there in 1979, the Reverend David Howell, now living in a retirement community. I called him. Of course, he did not remember standing outside with his arms crossed and his glasses blazing with blue. The first time I called him I forgot to ask him what he would have told me. When I called him back, he said it would depend on the circumstances, on where I was and where he was at that time. He did not think we are able to assert that there are any absolutes. I told him about the professor who advised me to do what Immanuel Kant did—just pick a metaphysical presumption in midair and build one's life around it. I thought that was as crazy as putting a brick in midair and building a house on it. David said that professors are not supposed to give religious answers.

Then I asked David the same question again, "And what would you have told me?" He said he might have asked me what my goals were and what was keeping me from attaining them. I told him that was the problem; I didn't have any goals. I wanted to know the absolute—the point of life—and give myself to that. That was my goal. Again, he said he doubted we could know anything absolutely and thought it rather arrogant to think so. After all these years, I discovered that the man with blue sky in his glasses probably would not have given me the answer I was longing to hear, though his kindness and his glasses did reflect the beauty of heaven. So, I thanked him and hung up.

Forty years later, the memory of the blue in his glasses had become bluer than the waters of the Bahamas where heaven fuses into the sea. Forty years of so much change, people coming and going, leaving home after home, death and life, had only made clearer the hallowed one, Christ, constant in the midst of my life, that way He sits on the chair over all, surrounded by a sea of lapis lazuli.

Acknowledgments

I thank the people of the Comunidad Cristiana de Fe in Medellín for putting up with a pastor who longs to be a poet for the past twenty-one years. I thank my wife, Kathy, for riding shotgun on my wagon hitched to a flaming vision. It has been a wild ride for almost thirty years living in Colombia and somehow she still looks good and has her hair in place. I thank my sons, Andrew Michael and Christian, who amaze me as much by their grace and wisdom as they are amazed how much I was an idiot growing up. Jesus made the difference in us all. Darlene Stern amazes me in her wisdom correcting the manuscript with the precision of a sharp shooter. I thought people praised their editors out of courtesy, but Noel Gruber and the team at Catch The Fire Books weaved my words into a flowing story. I also want to thank my dear friends and founders of our mission, Randy and Marcela MacMillan for loving and believing in me. Randy died on May 4, 2012, and left a blaze of bright colors behind in South America as a prophet, father and teacher who sketched the face of Christ with beautiful detail. Marcela bravely sails ahead into unchartered seas, singing.

About the Author

Andrew McMillan, with his wife Kathy, are the founding pastors of the Comunidad Cristiana de Fe in Medellín, Colombia. Andrew was born in Charleston, West Virginia, and majored in literature and religion at the University of Virginia, before receiving his Masters of Divinity from Yale Divinity School. Though wanting to be a poet, smoke a pipe, live near a pond and publish mildly famous books, Andrew ended up pastoring a Baptist church in New Jersey for six years. In 1986, shortly after getting married, Andrew and Kathy followed God to Colombia, where they served Pastor Randy MacMillan in Cali for seven years. In 1994 they planted Comunidad Cristiana de Fe in Medellín.

Today the church sees attendance of 8,000 people every weekend, with strong leadership, 850 home groups and 17 new church plants. Andrew's joy is seeing leaders having a blast together and pursuing the supernatural things of God. Andrew and Kathy have two adult sons, Andrew Michael and Christian, who both love God, love Colombia, and are studying in America.

You can find Andrew writing both poetry and theology at teammcmillan.org.

A God who
loves you

wants you to
experience him

be transformed

and given
power

At Catch The Fire, we are passionate about seeing people be transformed by a living God. We have many books that can help you on your journey, but we are also involved in much more.

Why not join us at a conference or seminar this year? Or come on a short-term mission with us? Or have your heart radically changed at a 5-month school. Or just visit one of our churches in many cities around the world.

CONTINUE YOUR JOURNEY AT

catchthefirebooks.com/whatsnext

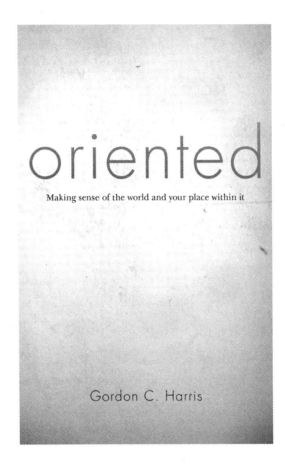

ORIENTED

GORDON C. HARRIS

Foreword by Bill Johnson

CONSUMED
BY LOVE

HOW ONENESS WITH CHRIST
CHANGES ABSOLUTELY EVERYTHING

DUNCAN SMITH

CONSUMED BY LOVE
DUNCAN SMITH

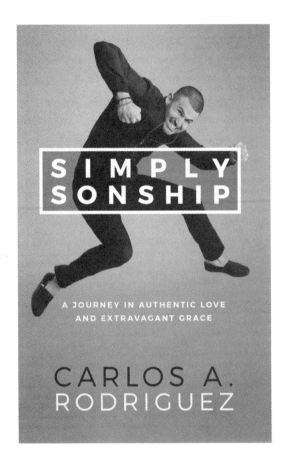

SIMPLY SONSHIP

CARLOS A. RODRIGUEZ

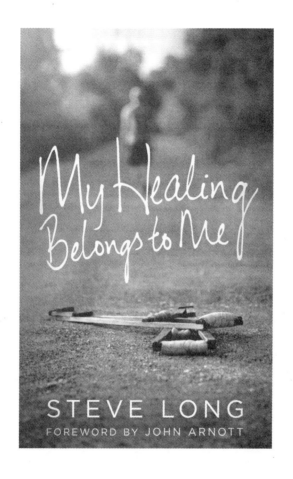

MY HEALING BELONGS TO ME
STEVE LONG